MACHIAVELLI OR THE DEMONIC CONFUSION

OLAVO DE CARVALHO

ASHMAN
FREE PRESS

To request permissions, contact the publisher at danielashman@protonmail.com.

Paperback ISBN: 978-1-7360306-0-8
Ebook ISBN: 978-1-7360306-1-5

First paperback edition October 2021.

Translated by Anthony Doyle
Indexed by Michael Hendry
Cover art by Arthur Angelo
Book layout by Brian Giles

This cover has been designed using resources from Freepik.com

Ashman Free Press
Boston, MA

AshmanFreePress.com

To my brother, Luiz Paulo de Carvalho.

CONTENTS

AUTHOR'S NOTE

THIS BOOK WAS a chapter of *The Revolutionary Mind* that grew too large and took on a life of its own. The same happened with various other chapters that split so pitilessly from the mother-cell and came out in separate volumes, such as *Descartes* and *The Cognitive Parallax*. This study on Machiavelli derives from notes I wrote for three lectures on the Political Philosophy course I gave to Public Administration students at the Catholic Pontifical University of Paraná in 2004. After going back over these notes and putting some finishing touches to them in 2009, I had the opportunity to read Sir Isaiah Berlin's essay *The Originality of Machiavelli*,[1] and saw that the idea of probing the meaning of Machiavelli's work through a historical review of its successive interpretations from the 16ᵗʰ Century to the present day had an illustrious precedent. However, as Berlin's aim was quite different to mine, my reading of this study, so informative in many aspects, yielded nothing which I felt needed to be incorporated into the conclusions of my own. Berlin was attempting to ascertain the meaning of Machiavelli's legacy "to us"; not what it meant to him and to his own life and times, but to other lives and other times that came after him. What interested me, on the other hand, was to peel back the various layers of often conflicting interpretations and uncover the original Machiavelli, stripped of all the pomp and exclamations of repugnance history had heaped upon him. Where Sir Isaiah Berlin had opted to add, I wished only to subtract.

Pursuant to his own method, the author of *The Originality of Machiavelli* found in the Florentine secretary a precursor of the liberal and democratic ideals he held so dear. However, he did recognize that this historical legacy was completely divorced from Machiavelli's own intentions and was but "a lucky irony of history." By all accounts, this was not the flesh and blood Machiavelli I was looking for, but one pasted together out of the reflected images and attributed intentions that so many admirers and detractors had spun for him, and not only out of erudite interpretations, but from the practical consequences they had drawn as precepts from his work. With more than just a whiff of Hegelian spirit, Sir Berlin had taken this historical compound as if it were the distilled essence of Machiavellian thought, revealed over the slow drip of historical process through its transmutation into its opposite. The problem with this method is that it fails to realize that the historical consequences that a work's influence engenders do not cease at any given time just because that period has been declared the final expression of its meaning. If, at this or that juncture, these repercussions may have crystallized into some more or less definitive form, it is very possible—and, in some cases, inevitable— that the sequence simply changes course the very next moment and ends up producing totally different effects. If Machiavelli was the unwitting prophet of liberal ideas and could be taken as such by Sir Isaiah Berlin in the 1970s, it is nigh-impossible today not to see in that same Machiavelli the voluntary and conscious harbinger of the highly bureaucratized and heavy-handed State which the American liberal democracy is fast becoming. The Machiavellian conception of the "Third Rome," which long hovered in the air as some hypothetical, unrealizable Utopia, is now taking on the semblance of a present, operative reality shaped by projects of centralized power which Saul Alinksy, the mentor of Barack Hussein Obama, seems to have copied straight out of the pages of Machiavelli's *Discourses on the First Decade of Titus Livy*.

On the other hand, while the Russian use of the "Third Rome" idea has nothing whatsoever to do with Machiavelli, the inspiration that the doctrinaire of the Russian Empire, Alexander Dugin, draws from his design for a resurgent Italy is patent. Just like Machiavelli's Italy, Dugin's Russia is a nation reduced to chaos, corruption, and impotence, and it's all the foreigners' fault. Unable to rebuild itself on its own steam, it must—Dugin contends— look to a system of alliances for support, one that can emerge from the destruction of its enemies as an Imperial power capable of dominating the whole world. The similarity to the Machiavellian plan of restoring Italy to its past glories could not be more evident.

What drove me to undertake this study was not to explore the succession of historical versions that have emerged of Machiavelli, but the opposite: to deconstruct that edifice, and ask to what extent Machiavelli himself was aware of the historical results he wanted to obtain. Without that deconstruction, we risk crowning as the supreme method of historical interpretation a mere archaeology of the projections other commentators and epochs have cast, often with ulterior motives, upon the author's own intentions.

My question is, therefore, this: How did Niccolò Machiavelli understand himself, and to what extent can we map, with relative certainty, the horizon of his consciousness? A horizon that defines itself not only by what it encompassed, but first and foremost by what it let slip its net. The plurality of contradictory interpretations of Machiavelli's thought emerges, at least in part, from the blind spots that appear in decisive articulations of that thought, and which turn certain developments attributed to him by interpreters and successors into little more than a metastasis of cancerous cells born of the prodigious mental confusion out of which they germinated.

Over the course of history, few thinkers have revealed themselves through so many blind spots in their visions of the world and of themselves as this study identifies in Machiavelli. With startling frequency, the Florentine fails to understand not only the events he explores, but himself and his own intentions, seeding his writings with unresolved and perhaps even unspotted contradictions. It is hardly surprising that a body of thought this nebulous and confusing, made yet more complex by a plethora of self-refutations and layers of camouflage, should have managed to generate such disparate and contradictory historical consequences.

Richmond, February 20, 2011

THE OBSCURITY OF MODERN PHILOSOPHY

DIFFICULTIES IN INTERPRETING philosophers have always existed. They arise more than ever when their work is written in dead languages, separated from the reader by the passage of time and not bridged by an unbroken, living tradition of reading and transmission. This was the case with certain works by Plato and Aristotle when they were restored to European culture in the 12th Century, with the added complication that they came to us incomplete. What remains of Aristotle is but a third of what he actually wrote, and it reaches us in the form of dashed-off, compressed, fragmentary class notes. Lost are the works he authorized for publication, by all accounts so clear and elegant that Cicero, judging them on their literary merits, described them as "a river of gold." Of Plato's output, we have a half or less. And, to make matters worse, he agreed to have only the most readily understandable parts of his thought committed to writing, reserving the best and most difficult teachings for oral exposition alone, and to only a handful of select disciples.

It is to be expected that, under such conditions, problems and errors of interpretation should abound. For centuries, readers have had to content themselves with a schematic overview of these philosophers' teachings, while an understanding of countless important details was left to the future. Advances in Philology only gradually managed to offer more exact reconstructions of the texts, comparisons with commentaries from the day and an approximate knowledge of the order of their writing, while efforts at philosophical interpretation coaxed out the intentions and unpicked the contradictions which the philosophers themselves had left unresolved. If the 20th Century did not establish a universal consensus, it certainly succeeded in whittling the difficulties of interpretation to one or two points of divergence that do not, however, substantially hamper a basic understanding of the two thinkers.

Even before that, however partial and insufficient the interpretations may have been, they were not marred by any serious misreading on the whole, and one still profits a great deal from studying Avicenna, Saint Thomas Aquinas and Francisco Suárez's commentaries on Aristotle, the works of the 17th-century Cambridge Platonists, and the Aristotelean investigations of Franz Brentano.

In short, we might say the modern intellectual world understood Aristotle and Plato well enough, and that this comprehension was steadily refined from Saint Thomas's first readings of the former in Latin translation (because he didn't know Greek) right up to the day Giovanni Reale, that master reader of the Ancients, managed to rebuild

Plato's famous "Unwritten Doctrine" by cross-matching first-hand testimonies and comparing them against the internal architecture of the system.[1]

Our experience of the modern philosophers, on the other hand, is altogether different. They don't write in dead languages, but in tongues generally spoken, and the reactions of their contemporaries are not unknown to us and don't have to be excavated from rare manuscripts, but are very well recorded for us in archives and libraries, when not published in widely-circulating books, often accompanied by the authors' own rebuttals and replies. The tradition of reading these authors and commenting on their work has been continuous over the centuries, giving us a clear vision of how the debate and *status quaestionis* have evolved. As for the original works themselves, we still have them and in faithful editions, too, as well as their authors' lesser works and even personal correspondence, annotated by patient philologists who decipher and elucidate each and every allusion made, person mentioned and opinion held in the day, all so painstakingly done that failing to understand the material can only be a matter of personal choice. Lastly, historical research has been able to piece together the biographies of each philosopher with enough acuity to, in the best cases, elucidate all the issues pertaining to their intellectual development and relationships with their social and cultural environments, and, in the worst, at least afford us more knowledge about their lives than we will ever possess about Aristotle and Plato.

However, despite all these guarantees, right from the outset the interpretation of many modern philosophers poses incomparably greater difficulties than readers of the philosophers of Antiquity, past or present, have had to contend with. These details do not concern the spiritual biographies of the figures in question, or what they may have thought on this or that particular issue, but the essential core of their philosophies, which would seem to permit various and antagonistic readings. A further difficulty is a direct result of that ambiguity, namely where each thinker should be categorized in the overall scheme of ideas, in the history of thought, and, last but not least, in the framework of the reader's own opinions and beliefs. It seems that many modern philosophers, unlike their forebears, are powerless against being cast and recast in whatever image the reader or critic deems fit, turning out over the generations, sometimes successively, often simultaneously, a democratic Machiavelli and an apologist for tyranny; a sincere, Christian Descartes and a masked anti-Christian; a Platonic, idealist Kant and a positivist materialist; a proto-Nazi Hegel and a Hegel as the herald of the State of Law; not to mention humanist and anti-humanist incarnations of Marx; Fascist and libertarian Nietzsches, and so on and so forth. These debates do not address mere issues of biographical or historical-cultural interest, but the very foundations, the vital cores of these philosophies, rendered all the more evanescent and ungraspable the deeper their interpreters probe. Amidst such a glut of documents and investigations, the reader's intellect finds itself facing a deplorable dearth of actual understanding.

Lastly, we arrive at the most disturbing detail of all. Two of the philosophers who wrote the most, left reams of unfinished, unorganized work behind them, wrestled with the hardest subjects the human mind has ever endeavored to address, and never had the chance, desire, or aspiration to organize their ideas into an all-encompassing system (with the aggravating factor that one of them changed his intellectual orientation on numerous occasions throughout his lifetime) are, nonetheless, those who pose to this day the fewest difficulties of interpretation. I am referring to Leibniz and Schelling. Leibniz died in 1716, but some of his most important works did not make it out of the drawer until the late 19th Century. As for the serious interpretations of his oeuvre, these only began with Bertrand Russell's *A Critical Exposition of the Philosophy of Leibniz* in 1900 and L. Couturat's *La Logique de Leibniz* the following year. As for Schelling, his academic career came to an unfortunate end, as his major works, especially *Philosophy of Mythology* and *Philosophy of Revelation*, written in later life, met with little interest among his peers. These two works would only receive the attention they deserved decades later. And yet, such obstacles notwithstanding, no-one could deny that we now have a clear enough understanding of the thinking of these two great philosophers, and, in the case of Schelling, even of his complex evolution as a thinker. We see no differences of interpretation here, none of the 180-degree about-turns we get with Machiavelli or Nietzsche.

What this shows beyond a shadow of a doubt is that the difficulties of reaching consensus on the interpretation of many modern philosophers is not extrinsic, but intrinsic. It is not that we, the readers, struggle to understand them, but that they are badly explained or riven with unresolved and perhaps unnoticed internal contradictions (which would imply not even their authors had a clear grasp of their own meaning), or perhaps harbor deep within some mystery of another nature.

Why is it so absolutely necessary to decipher this mystery, or at least attempt to formulate it in an explicit manner as a well-defined problem?

First of all, as modernity presents itself and indeed proclaims itself the age of "enlightenment"—*Erklärung, Esclarecimento, l'Âge des Lumières*—, the hero that drew back the veil of darkness that had clouded the vision of previous generations, it is simply impermissible that it should be allowed to leave such a muddled, shaded account of itself.

Secondly, while its successor, post-modernism, brags of having "deconstructed" the complex structures of modern thought and revealed all its cogs and springs, it does so through a discourse even more impenetrable and obscure, so much so that leading lights of this movement within the upper echelons of academia have proved incapable of distinguishing their own discourse from the dadaist parody made of it by the physicist Alan Sokal.[2] The historical record shows that such a prodigious level of unintelligibility has rarely been attained.

Thirdly and lastly, it is important because philosophers have never enjoyed such power to influence the course of society and history than they have since the onset of modernity, an age that has catapulted them almost to the station of rulers or prophets. Never have the destinies of multitudes and even the private feelings and personal fantasies of the common man been so directly influenced by the doctrines of philosophers, whose thinking proliferates swiftly among the "academic proletariat" on university campuses, in the mass media and on the internet, invading homes and minds—conscious and perhaps even subconscious—and quickly establishing themselves as forces capable of shaping the lives of millions. Today, more than ever before, it is crucial that the reader of the history of philosophy know that *de te fabula narratur.*[3] This history is the history of our lives. Unless we understand it, we won't understand ourselves.

2

IMAGE OF MACHIAVELLI

OF THE MOST RENOWNED modern philosophers, Niccolò Machiavelli is perhaps the first to present the reader with such an ambiguous and puzzling doctrine. So ambiguous and puzzling that one of its greatest interpreters, Benedetto Croce, summed up four centuries of investigations with the disheartening conclusion that the Florentine thinker is "an enigma we shall never unravel." After Croce, other first-rate scholars, such as Leo Strauss, Quentin Skinner, Hans Baron and Maurizio Viroli, thought they had found the key to the riddle, but their solutions were so radically different from one another that they served only to compound it.

I certainly do not hope to enjoy any more success in my endeavor than these illustrious thinkers. I confess from the outset that I do not understand Machiavelli any more clearly than they, and perhaps even less. But my goal here is not to explain Machiavelli; merely to explain his inexplicability. My plan is to draft the profile of his unintelligibility more precisely, because it has been so thoroughly incorporated into half a millennium of philosophical and political discussion in the West that it is no exaggeration to consider it one of the few constants of modernity. Not wanting to leap to the conclusion before I have stated the problem, let me just throw down the following startling phenomenon: one of the first philosophical icons of modernity is an author that modernity itself admits it does not understand. Machiavelli's ideas do not stay on the page, nor are they content simply to father other ideas: they transmogrify into ambitions and acts, inspire coups d'état and revolutions, found nations and political regimes, but still we don't comprehend them. I would ask the reader to bear that in mind as we go forward, because we will return to it in due course. For now, however, let us see how all the confusion began.

§

The first reactions to Machiavelli's *The Prince* created the popular image of the author as a cynical immoralist, a theorist of mendacity and political violence, an apologist for tyrants and, as Leo Strauss put it, "a teacher of evil." Even among the author's friends there were some who turned away from him in disgust. Francesco Vettori, his close friend and confidante, the man who had helped Machiavelli win back the bureaucratic post he had been stripped of after the fall of the Florentine Republic he had served from 1498 to 1512, delicately withdrew all further support in the wake of such literary knavery. A witness from the time noted: "Everyone hated him because of *The*

Prince. The decent found him a scoundrel, and the scoundrels, even worse than they."[1]

The scandal crossed borders, too. In England, Cardinal Reginald Pole denounced Machiavelli as a "Satanic spirit, defender of despotism and justifier of all manners of violence."[2] William Shakespeare branded him in verse as "the murderous Machiavelli."

The succession of condemnations culminated at the Council of Trent, in 1564, which saw *The Prince* added to the *Index librorum prohibitorum* first compiled by Pope Paul IV five years earlier.

But Machiavelli's posthumous flagellation was only beginning. The terms "Machiavellian" and "Machiavellism" embarked on a long and successful career in the universal vocabulary of infamy when, in 1576, the French patriot Innocent Gentillet used the term in reference to "the Italianized French"—Catherine de Medici and her court—, who he blamed for the Saint Bartholomew's Day massacre of the (protestant) Huguenots in 1572.

Seen from this perspective, Machiavelli was an apostle of *Raison d'État*, which, in the name of national grandeur and security, entitles rulers to lie, cheat, steal, oppress, kill, and break every church commandment and wider moral law.

Even an unwavering believer in *Raison d'État*, the French thinker Jean Bodin, a far more competent philosopher than Machiavelli, felt compelled to reject his rival's unilateral amorality, noting that, in the structure of state power, there was—and had to be—a constant creative tension between a monarch's freedom to act and his or her duty to uphold the laws of morality and religion. Based on this understanding, he lambasted Machiavelli as a spirit at once *levissimus et nequissimus* (frivolous and vicious).[3]

The following century a man none would ever have accused of political naivety, Frederick II of Prussia, wrote his *Anti-Machiavelli* to "defend humanity against the monster who would destroy it."[4] Voltaire, who ought to have been more than pleased by the Florentine's attacks on religion, opted, out of sheer obsequiousness, to subscribe to the thesis preferred by his patron, the Emperor.

§

It did not take long for discordant voices to raise radical objections against the general consensus. In 1585, Alberico Gentilli, an Italian refugee in England, where he taught Civil Law at Oxford, published a fervent defense of Machiavelli in his treatise *De Legacionibus*,[5] which not only presented the Florentine as an erudite, honest sage, but vehemently contested the prevailing view that branded him an advocate of tyranny. As Gentilli understood it, Machiavelli was nothing less than...wait for it: a republican and steadfast democrat. It was all, he claimed, slander based on misunderstanding. *The Prince* was not a treatise of immorality, but a work of moral criticism; not a playbook for tyrants, but a cruel and steadfast portrait of tyranny. By dressing up an unflinching description of how princes actually behaved as advice for how they ought to conduct themselves, the book blew the lid off their tenebrous strategies and so armed the people with the antidote.

Though grounded upon a reading that inverted the

literal sense of Machiavelli's text, the interpretation that he was a "misunderstood republican" was accepted by many illustrious figures.[6] Lord Bacon adhered without hesitation. Baruch de Spinoza, in his *Tractatus Politicus*, praised the author of *The Prince* as a "wise man" who not only defended liberty, but "gave healthy counsel as to how best to preserve it." And from Spinoza, this version sprang straight into Pierre Bayle's *Historical and Critical Dictionary* and Denis Diderot's *Encyclopedia*, cementing it as prevailing opinion among the Enlightenment thinkers (Voltaire excepted). In his *Social Contract*, Rousseau wrote: "While appearing to instruct kings, Machiavelli did much to educate the people. His *The Prince* is a book for republicans." The historian and abolitionist leader Thomas Babington Macaulay (1800-1859) not only confirmed Machiavelli's republicanism, but cast him as a hero of freedom and paragon of political morality. In his famous essay published in the March 1827 issue of *The Edinburgh Review*, he writes:

> We doubt whether it would be possible to find, in all the many volumes of his composition, a single expression indicating that dissimulation and treachery had ever struck him as desirable...We are acquainted with few writings which exhibit so much elevation of sentiment, so pure and warm a zeal for the public good, or so just a view of the duties and rights of citizens, as those of Machiavelli.

§

With the advent of naturalistic social science in the 19th Century, these reactions were impugned, some as the untoward intrusions of Christian morality upon the field of politics, others as just youthful outbursts of republican enthusiasm. They were replaced by a sterilized version of Machiavellism as an attempt to depict political reality with cold objectivity, "devoid of value judgements." Machiavelli's politics was not immoral, merely amoral or extra-moral, as all positivist science should be.

In the introduction to his famous critical edition of *The Prince*, Lord Lawrence Arthur Burd wrote that:

> the creation of the new method [of political science] was by no means the work of Machiavelli alone; it was the product of a whole set of Italian publicists, of which Machiavelli and Guicciardini were but the most famous. All of them, even when they did not expressly state their method of investigation, were clearly not arguing, as Aquinas would have it, '*secundum Scripturae divinae auctoritatem, Philosophorum dogmata et exempla laudatorum Principum*,'[7] but stick to experience and eschew speculations wafting about 'on the air.'[8]

This image of Machiavelli as a "precursor" to the social science of Durkheim and Weber continued to attract supporters right into the mid-1900s. Ernst Cassirer, for example, wrote:

> The Prince is neither a moral nor immoral book; it is simply a technical book. In a technical book we do not seek rules of ethical conduct, of good and evil. It is

enough if we are told what is useful and useless. Every word in *The Prince* must be read and interpreted in this way. The book contains no moral prescripts for the ruler nor does it invite him to commit crimes and villainies. It is especially concerned with and destined for the 'new principalities.' It tries to give them all the advice necessary for protecting themselves from all danger...Machiavelli studied political actions in the same way as a chemist studies chemical reactions. Assuredly a chemist who prepares in his laboratory a strong poison is not responsible for its effects... Machiavelli's *Prince* contains many dangerous and poisonous things, but he looks at them with the coolness and indifference of a scientist. He gives his political prescriptions.[9]

The passage above is from *The Myth of the State*, written in 1944 and published posthumously in 1946. Olschki, as the following passage from Carpeaux shows, was in full agreement:

in his book *Machiavelli the Scientist* (Berkeley, 1948), Olschki compares the new science of man, Machiavelli's science, with the new science of nature, Galileo's: neither one nor the other studied the 'why' or 'for what' of things, merely the 'how.' Is that the key to Machiavelli's so-called immoralism? Yet nobody considers Galileo's falling objects immoral just because the great physicist failed to factor into his discovery the possibility that a falling object might hit and kill someone. Machiavelli was simply studying the laws of human behavior in public

life, without concerning himself with moral conclusions.
He is a scientist.[10]

§

If the reader is keeping tally, that's three Machiavellis
already—the immoralist, the democrat, and the scientist.
None of these encompasses the other two, or can be
readily reduced to either. But now things get really
complicated. Almost simultaneously with Machiavelli the
Scientist a fourth Florentine arises, Machiavelli the
Patriot, created by a series of revolutions that culminated
in the creation of the independent Italian state in 1861,
thanks to Giuseppe Garibaldi, the Count Camilo di
Cavour, and the king of Piemonte-Sardenha, Vittorio
Emanuele II, the first ruler of the united Italy. On the spur
of nationalist enthusiasm, Niccolò's work was re-read in a
key that placed its core inspiration squarely on the desire
to unify the nation, fragmented into five autonomous principalities, and, expelling the French oppressors, emulate
much of the rest of Europe by a creating a nation state.
Pasquale Villari, Machiavelli's first great biographer,
subscribes wholeheartedly to this thesis. All the disparate
aspects of the author's work—ruthless villainies, real or
apparent; nostalgia for Ancient Rome; criticisms of the
Church; pertinent observations and pejorative distortions
—were but components in a persuasion machine designed
for patriotic ends:

> When, completing his analysis, Machiavelli finally states
> his conclusions, we see the practical aspect and real aim

of the work plainly expounded. The goal is to bring about the unity of the Italian Patria and free it from the foreign yoke.[11]

This interpretation could perhaps be discarded as mere pamphletary, were it not for two key factors:

The first is that it was quite recently legitimized by one of the most respected authorities on the subject, Maurizio Viroli, and with some very solid reasons to back it up, as we shall see further on.

The second is that Benito Mussolini, in his drive to push Italian nationalism to its extremes in the early 20th Century, turned Machiavelli's thought into one of the pillars of the Fascist doctrine, with the difference that he did not only absorb its patriotism, as had the revolutionaries of 1861, but the very meat of its morality, its vision of the state, and approach to governance, forming an inseparable theoretical-practical synthesis akin to that which emerges from Machiavelli's work itself. Il Duce's enthusiasm for the Renaissance thinker knows no bounds. He wrote about it for the first time in the article titled "Nationalism," published in the newspaper *La Lotta di Classi*, in which he called for the formation of a national army—one of the Florentine secretary's classic arguments. He would return to the issue in *Popolo d'Italia* on March 26, 1915, railing against the threadbare state of the national spirit in language that could well have been lifted straight from *The Prince*, but here also vaguely ascribing to the Jews the same blame Machiavelli had leveled against the Catholic Church. In a speech delivered at the Teatro Communale in Bologna on March 19, 1918, Mussolini claimed that the boldness and *Virtù* (will power) Machiavelli celebrates in his princes apply just as truly to the people as a whole (an idea also latent in Machiavelli himself). On March 3, 1922, Il Duce lamented that Machiavelli was "the least read and least practiced of all Italian writers."[12] In 1924, Mussolini wrote a famous preface to *The Prince* and, in 1935, helped distribute the book on a wide scale through cheap, state-sponsored editions.[13] But none of this was pure propaganda: he truly meditated on Machiavelli's teachings, tweaked to suit the times. Mussolini was many things, but a shoddy interpreter of Machiavelli he was not. When he equates the Prince with the State, he shows that he had understood the master's lesson very well indeed, according to which the amoralism of government was not a separate doctrinal aspect, but the practical expression of nationalism in action, which, in turn, incarnated the State as a sovereign entity, itself personified in the figure of its ruler. His idea of national militias follows the Machiavellian project to the letter, while his conception of the State as an entity above the Church, and of permanent conflict between the individual and the State are also pure Machiavelli.[14]

Mussolini's genuine affinity with and understanding of Machiavelli's thought didn't go unnoticed, even by his most implacable enemies. As early as 1922, the Catholic militant Vito G. Galati was flagging the Machiavellian inspiration in fascism in his study *L'Ombra di Macchiavelli* (Machiavelli's Shadow). In October 1933, Leon Trotsky wrote an article called "What is National Socialism?", published in the journal *The Modern Thinker*:

> Mussolini from the very beginning reacted more consciously to social materials than Hitler, to whom the police mysticism of a Metternich is much closer than the political algebra of Machiavelli. Mussolini is mentally bolder and more cynical.[15]

Hitler and Stalin are two other notorious dictators who drew inspiration from Machiavelli. I don't think it can be mere coincidence that both men, and indeed also Mussolini, associated Machiavelli's suggested manner of ruling with a cult of State, and, moreover, an extreme breed of nationalism. "Extreme nationalism" is the very definition of national socialism, such that one of Stalin's most ingenious—indeed, Machiavellian—achievements as a strategist and propagandist was to have known just how to reconcile the administrative internationalism of the communist movement with the intensely patriotic cult to Mother Russia, and to do so only a few years after Lenin had declared nationalism one of communism's deadliest enemies—a conclusion that seemed eminently justifiable at the time.

At the end of the day, Machiavelli the immoralist and Machiavelli the patriot aren't as different as they might appear. At least in practice, where Machiavellian opportunism erases differences as it sees fit. For the scholar, however, there is still the problem—and an essential one at that—of ascertaining which of the two plays the subordinate role. If the immoralism is a means and the patriotism the end, as Villari claims, Machiavelli's demonic airs are attenuated somewhat. However, if the patriotism is the minor chord, a mere cog in a mechanism designed to oust the Christian God in favor of a historical and terrestrial divinity, then we're not even talking about immoralism here, but something much worse.

§

However, before the scholars could clearly formulate this dilemma, the onward march of the history of art and culture in the first half of the 20th Century produced a fifth Machiavelli, just to complicate matters even further. The amoralism of Machiavelli's politics was not scientific in its inspiration, but artistic. This new interpretation, derived from Benedetto Croce's rigid distinction between ethics and politics (the realm of the "good" and the realm of the "useful"),[16] turned Machiavelli into a technocrat, a neutral counsellor throwing himself into the design of the State with the artist's pure love of formal perfection, with no thought whatsoever for the consequences: it was technique for technique's sake, art for the sake of art. Launched by the Italian scholar Luigi Russo, the thesis was defended brilliantly by Lauro Escorel:

> He went so far as to adopt a complete detachment in the face of the political crisis of his world, believing that he could resolve it in the same way as one builds a great work of art. He was a man of the Renaissance, homo aestheticus, as 'amoral' as a poet for whom only the perfection of his verses matters; but this poet was borne out by history. Politically and historically speaking, Machiavelli is right; though morally, his position is unconscionable. Taking Benedetto Croce's

rigorous separation of the political and moral as his base, Luigi Russo proposes a solution to the Machiavelli problem—perhaps the only solution possible—and finds in Mr. Lauro Escorel an adherent: Machiavelli's theory is irrefutable as political doctrine, but there is more to the world of human interactions than politics, and our fates are wrought of more than just political solutions. The Machiavellism of Machiavelli is a technique of means that ignores the ends. At its core, it is a 'pure' technique with no finality whatsoever, just like works of art. And that is why it is defined by a multiplicity of possible meanings. It is ambiguous, as are all major artworks.[17]

§

All of these interpretations have their grain of truth: in Machiavelli's politics we find elements of despotic immoralism, of democratic republicanism, of patriotism, of cold description and artistic idealization. And over the centuries, illustrious readers who have stopped short of creating an interpretation to call their own have opted to emphasize this or that aspect and so angle Machiavelli as something of a precursor to their own work. German nationalism, for example, readily assumed the shape of a cult to the abstract idea of the State in the wake of Hegel, hence the historian Treitschke, himself a fervent patriot, exulted Machiavelli's role in pioneering the idea. Machiavelli, he says, "was a powerful thinker who cooperated with Martin Luther in liberating the State."[18] By 'liberating the State' read 'releasing nascent nation States from the shackles of supranational authority,' whether of the Medieval Empire or the Catholic Church.

Along similar lines, and with no nationalist preaching in mind, another German historian correctly notes that the immoralist pragmatism of *Raison d'État* was by no means unknown in Antiquity. What was new was the fact that Machiavelli had raised this doctrine to a more general and abstract level: "Altogether the ancient conception of *raison d'état* remained at this time firmly fixed in personalities, and served to vindicate the mode of action which was forced on contemporary rulers by the pressure of the situation. It never seemed to rise (or at least not at all consistently) towards the conception of a supra-individual and independent state personality, which would stand over and against the actual rulers of the time."[19] As Treitschke said, Machiavelli was the first to realize clearly that power is the stuff of the State.

Friedrich Nietzsche, on the other hand, saw Machiavelli as the precursor of his own ideas on the corrosive influence of the Christian ethic, which both saw as having been responsible for the "degeneration" of the European peoples.[20]

§

However, when so many disparate elements cluster without managing to form a coherent pattern, human intelligence can't resist the impulse to rearrange it all in search of some unseen formal nexus that might confer order on the mess. That's what the revolutionary ideologue Antonio Gramsci did with Machiavelli. For Gramsci, Machiavellism was not an apology for immorality or despotism, or for democracy for that matter, nor was it a description of reality, nor a patriotic appeal, much less *art pour l'art*. As he saw it, it was a little of all of that compacted into a very long-term action plan. The Prince didn't exist: Machiavelli was portraying him much as one would in a ritual designed to invoke the envisioned and summon it into existence—if not immediate existence, at least in some future time. Shortly before Gramsci, one of his masters, the critic Francesco de Sanctis, author of the acclaimed *Storia della Letteratura Italiana*, exclaimed:

> [Machiavelli's plan] is the project of a modern world, developed, corrected, expanded and more or less executed. Great is the nation that saw [him] arise. We should therefore be proud of our Machiavelli. Glory to him wheresoever part of the old world crumbles! And glory to him whenever another part is added to the new![21]

But let us not confuse matters. For Gramsci, Machiavelli was no "prophet," in the sense of a clairvoyant foretelling the future. He does not "foresee" this future, but plans it and strives to bring it about through the intellectual influence he exercises over a ruler (in *The Prince*) and over two would-be rulers (in *The Discourses*).[22] Some interpreters have tried to limit the reach of this plan to the immediate circumstances of his native Italy. But that can only be said of *The Prince*. In *The Discourses*, he sketches the far more ambitious project of a Third Rome (we will return to this later on), the model for an entirely new society, the creation of which would have transcended beyond measure any solution to the Italian problem.[23] It is the "project of a modern world" to which de Sanctis referred. According to Villari, the unification of Italy could only be brought about by a "reformer Prince, and by the [technocratically amoral] means suggested and imposed by history and experience." The wider plan for a Third Rome, as Antonio Gramsci saw it, required something more. No individual governor would be equal to the task, at least not completely. It would take an elite council, a vanguard conscious of the global revolution. In other words, it would take the Party of Lenin and Gramsci. If Machiavelli is a prophet, it is not in the vulgar sense of a seer, but in the etymological sense of the Greek verb *prophero*: to order, have something done, make something happen.[24] Machiavelli saw himself as a new Moses parting the Red Sea of politics, paving the way towards the promised land of the Third Rome. And without wielding any political power himself, he would fulfill this role through intellectual leadership, through the written word.

§

By this stage, Machiavelli's reputation among the literati was much better than it had been in the 16th century. Dissolved in successive baths of extenuating factors—republicanism, patriotism, science, art, prophecy —, Machiavelli's immoralism seemed to have withdrawn to the realm of folk belief, sedimented as the kind of lore the scholar can't be seen to take seriously. And it was right then that one highly competent scholar decided to take it all extremely seriously indeed. What led Leo Strauss to consider this hypothesis anew was his own personal experience. As a Jew who had escaped the clutches of the Nazis, he knew very well that not everything a philosopher thinks can be committed to writing. Very often the written word is used to hide rather than express a thought. In the case of Machiavelli, the suspicion was particularly justified because he had confessed as much to Francesco Vettori:

> For some time I never say what I believe and I never believe what I say; and if it sometimes occurs to me that I say the truth, I conceal it among so many lies that it is hard to find it out.[25]

It is probably the most shocking confession in all of world history. And once aware of it, no-one can really ignore Strauss' warning that many philosophical works can have two layers of meaning: an "exoteric" meaning for the masses, and an "esoteric" meaning for the happy few who are not afraid of tremendous truths (or lies). Strauss had used this criterion with reasonable success in his reading of Maimonides and Spinoza, and his reason for doing so again with Machiavelli is not restricted to the confession above:

> Machiavelli's work is rich in manifest blunders of various kinds: misquotations, misstatements regarding names or events, hasty generalizations, indefensible omissions, and so on. It is a rule of common prudence to "believe" that all these blunders are intentional and in each case to raise

the question as to what the blunder might be meant to signify.[26]

The results of applying this "rule of common prudence" to Machiavelli are frightening: the superficial immoralism of his advice to the Prince, cushioned, in turn, under a layer of apparently moralizing exhortations, is just a façade to disguise a much deeper attack on religion, conceived in such a manner as to rope his readers into a blasphemous reasoning without their having any idea of the kind of guilt they are shouldering by following the author in his counsel.

§

In the meantime, new arguments also arose to support old hypotheses. The figure of the camouflaged republican returned stronger than ever thanks to the American historian Garrett Mattingly, who argued that *The Prince* is not so much an apology for tyrants as a satire of them.

> I suppose it is possible to imagine that a man who has seen his country enslaved, his life's work wrecked and his career with it, and has, for good measure, been tortured within an inch of his life should thereupon go home and write a book intended to teach his enemies the proper way to maintain themselves, writing all the time, remember, with the passionless objectivity of a scientist in a laboratory. It must be possible to imagine such behavior, because Machiavelli scholars do imagine it and

accept it without a visible tremor. But it is a little difficult for the ordinary mind to compass.[27]

Besides the unlikelihood of the situation, Mattingly also pinpoints some flagrant incoherencies that would seem to impugn a literal reading:

> Only in a satire can one understand the choice of Cesare Borgia as the model prince. The common people of Tuscany could not have had what they could expect of a prince's rule made clearer than by the example of this bloodstained buffoon whose vices, crimes, and follies had been the scandal of Italy, and the conduct of whose brutal, undisciplined troops had so infuriated the Tuscans that when another band of them crossed their frontier, the peasants fell upon them and tore them to pieces.[28]

But if the thesis of a republican and democratic Machiavelli has gained favor among historians in recent decades, those who adhere to it often do so on the grounds of arguments that run in a very different direction to Mattingly's. Disagreeing with Strauss's reading on this level at least, Quentin Skinner argues that it is wrong to look for any coherence of thought over time in Machiavelli's work. For Skinner, between *The Prince* and *The Discourses*, the author had simply changed his mind. Which would imply, evidently, that Machiavelli had written both in all sincerity. Presenting hard evidence that Machiavelli's *modus arguendi* was never scientific, but rhetorical (in diametric opposition to the interpretation of

Cassirer, Max Lerner and others), Maurizio Viroli looks at *The Prince* and *The Discourses* as patriotic exhortations.[29] From this perspective, neither work could have been a satire.

These and many other partial additions were made to the increasingly enigmatic portrait of Machiavelli.

3

MACHIAVELLI'S PSEUDO-REALISM

As explained above, it is not my intention to resolve the enigma, merely to parse its elements so as to stress its importance as a staple of Western intellectual history since the 16th Century.

To that end, we might take as a starting point Antonio Gramsci's incontestable observation that, if *The Prince* consists of elements gleaned from the typical behaviors of the Italian politicians of the day, then what interested the Florentine was not the reality as such, but what he could make of it. Machiavelli had no political power himself with which to bring whatever plan he drafted to fruition, only the weaponry of the intellectual: the power of the written word. Curiously, it was a power he disdained, as he did all those who used it, a point on which, according to Strauss, he was of a view with Socrates, whose realism attacked the boundless confidence the sophists had in the power of discourse as an instrument of social transformation.[1] Nothing, Machiavelli insists, is a match for military might. However, once again, this bellicosity refers to the lie of the political land and to the figure of the Prince, not to his prophet, Machiavelli himself. What the author was casting into the waters of the future here was the hook of discourse, with which he hoped to fish to the surface the new era lying in wait on the seafloor of possibility. Bringing that possibility about would have required a knowledge of the laws of historical necessity, and Machiavelli boasted of being the first to possess that knowledge (we will get to what that was in a while) and the skills to unpack its novel prospects for mankind. Not just its promise of theoretical knowledge, but the possible creation of a new world.

In this sense, he foresees the operation which Hegel[2] would describe in the following terms:

> Every individual is a blind link in the chain of absolute necessity, along which the world develops. Every individual can raise himself to domination (*Herrschaft*) over a great length of this chain only if he realizes the goal of this great necessity and, by virtue of this knowledge, learns to speak the magic words (*die Zauberworte*) which evoke its shape (*Gestalt*).

Analyzing this fragment, Eric Voegelin does not see in Hegel a philosopher attempting to describe the structure of reality so much as a conjurer or sorcerer intent on molding it in the image of some hypothetical future:

> For Hegel betrays in so many words that being a mere man is not enough for him; and, as he cannot be the

divine Lord of history himself, he is going to achieve
Herrschaft as a sorcerer who will conjure up an image of
history—a shape, a ghost—that is meant to eclipse the
history of God's making. The imaginative project of
history falls in its place in the pattern of modern
existence as the conjurer's instrument of power.[3]

Strange as it may seem, Voegelin does not make the
same judgement of Machiavelli, though the analysis
would fit equally well. Rather, albeit in a text intentionally
left unpublished, he described him as "a healthy and
honest figure, certainly preferable as a man to the contrac-
tualists (above all Locke) who try to cover the reality of
power underneath [...] the immoral swindle of consent."[4]
Voegelin goes so far as to grace him with the title "spiritual
realist," right up there with Plato and Aristotle, Thomas
Aquinas, Leibniz and Schelling. For the Louisiana
philosopher, the spiritual realist is the thinker who has an
appropriate understanding of man's place in the structure
of reality and does not confuse immanence with transcen-
dence, and so nurtures no illusions as to the perfectibility
of this world. Though Voegelin later abandoned the use of
this concept and, according to his disciple Dante Germino,
revised his assessment of Machiavelli,[5] the truth remains
that, strictly in terms of comparison with the idealist falsification of reality, the judgement was far from inadequate.
If there is one thing Machiavelli cannot be accused of it is
of hiding power relations beneath an enchanted veil or of
investing all his hopes in a future society freed of repres-
sion and terror. Quite the contrary, his Third Rome is
entirely founded upon fear of authority. Later, Voegelin

himself would admit that that was not enough to classify Machiavelli as a "spiritual realist" and even recognized in the Florentine a pronounced "demonic" streak that, if it did not contradict his judgement on that particular point, certainly modified his overall assessment of him. Voegelin died before he could explain that change at any length, and I do not intend to wager what it might have been. What does strike me as clear, however, is that his realist pessimism as to the world's perfectibility is entirely compatible with Machiavelli's aim of bringing about a new world through words of command put into the mouths of future princes by a resurrected Moses. And, if I see no escaping the conclusion that, in this, he was a predecessor of Hegel's work of sorcery, it is precisely because he is in no way a new Moses, but, as we shall see, an anti-Moses, his inversion, a secular parody of the Hebrew prophet.

4

PARODY OF PROPHECY

THIS IS WORTH examining in more detail.

1. Machiavelli never denies the existence of God, the prophetic power invested in Moses by Divine Providence, or the presence of a divine influx throughout the later expansion of Christianity. All of this falls, for Machiavelli, under the concept of "Fortune" (*Fortuna*), the set of destiny-determining factors that lie beyond human control. Fortune stands over and against "*Virtù*," which is not to be confused with virtue in a moral or religious sense, as it refers here to will to power, decisiveness, and capacity to act, especially the skillset displayed by the true leader, the princes of this world.

For Machiavelli, Ancient Rome was born from the *Virtù* of its founders, but it succumbed to corruption and allowed itself to mollify under the corrosive influence of the son of God and the Judeo-Christian tradition, in other words, of *Fortuna*. The Second Rome, the Rome of the

Popes, arose out of Judeo-Christendom, and its enviable power lay in raveling the fibers of conquered nations with the ruinous influence of a doctrine of resignation and compassion. For Machiavelli, therein lay the root of all the woes befalling the European peoples in general and the Italians in particular. The liberation of Italy, in the short term, and the creation of the Third Rome, at some unde-fined future time, would have to stem from the triumph of *Virtù* over *Fortuna,* with all the decrees of Providence repealed by a tremendous act of power.

Machiavelli believed in free will, and he appealed to man to use it against God. There is therefore no way he did not know, as he donned the robes of Moses, that he was doing so in the skin of an anti-Moses. The parodic inversion could not be clearer.

And with this, all the airbrushed images of Machi-avelli the Scientist and Machiavelli the Artist go straight into the trash can, as do the naive criticisms that branded the Florentine bureaucrat a vulgar immoralist. The evidence leaves little doubt that to give "Machiavellian" counsel to princes is to sin against all morality, but to invest oneself with prophetic authority in order to thwart Providence and attempt to reverse the divine course of History goes way beyond "immorality." It's not even polit-ical perversion. It is metaphysical rebellion, a sin against the Holy Spirit.

2. The parodic nature of the undertaking becomes all the clearer when we examine it chronologically. Up until 1513, Machiavelli (born in 1469) had written only admin-istrative documents of little consequence. *The Prince*, penned that same year, came four years before the

Discorsi sopra la prima deca di Tito Livio (*Discourses on the First Decade of Titus Livius*), six before *Vita di Castruccio Castracani* (*The Life of Castruccio Castracani*), eight before *Arte della guerra* (*The Art of War*), and twelve before his *Istorie Fiorentine* (*Florentine Histories*). Clearly, the Machiavellian conception of government, with the prophecy of the advent of the Reformer Prince, was primed and ready the very moment its author created, retroactively, a global interpretation of History to justify it. His interpretation of the past is pre-molded by his foreglimpse of the future. This curious reversal of the structure of time is common, almost without exception, to the thinkers who marked the modern cycle: Hobbes, Locke, Kant, Hegel, August Comte, Karl Marx, and even Nietzsche. Without standing on the slightest ceremony, each believed he had seen the future and took that vision as the premise upon which to explain the past. It's a phenomenon I call *pseudo-propheticism*, and it's a structural characteristic of modern thought, and especially so of the revolutionary mentality, in the explicit sense in which I use the term.

3. Even more interesting is the relationship that exists between the two major works, *The Prince* and *The Discourses*, and the function they served in kickstarting Machiavelli's own political career. *The Prince* is dedicated to Lorenzo de Medici, the ruling prince, and it speaks, above all, of principalities. *The Discourses*, on the other hand, takes republics as the central theme, and is dedicated to two private citizens with ambitions to rule. Naturally, the prophet tries to hedge his bets against any unexpected blips along the way towards the fulfillment of

his prophecy. His vision of the future can serve to guide a drastic reinterpretation of History as a whole, but not as the sole rudder of Machiavelli's own career. The Third Rome is an absolute certainty, even more firmly established than the past—as is its function, in fact—, but we still don't know if Rome 3.0 will come in the form of a principality or a republic. So perhaps the best thing to do is prepare for both possibilities, fawning in equal measure over the two types of leader. Prophesying for wider humanity is one thing, but greater care must be taken when dealing with one's own personal future. Just imagine if Moses, pointing the way across the Red Sea, had hedged his faith in the parting of the waves with a rental boat, just in case. In displaying awareness of this distinction, our new Moses, like Don Quixote, proves himself to be *loco sí, pero no tonto* (Crazy, yes; but not dumb).

5

THE LIAR

IF THIS STRIKES you as a shade circuitous and dishonest, it's hardly surprising: "*I never say what I believe and I never believe what I say.*" The words make Machiavelli, and by his own admission, the very incarnation of the "liar's paradox" and places the reader immediately at the heart of a problem I have taken to calling "existential self-reference": is the liar telling the truth at the moment of his confession, or is he lying about everything that went before? Has he really led a life of lies, or is he lying about the kind of life he has led? His interpreters soon realized that it was impossible to understand Machiavelli without elucidating the exact relationship between the actual meaning of his text and the unspoken truth of his existence. They came to a hodgepodge of conclusions, but four key personal details from Machiavelli's life and work should not be forgotten:

1. The man who judged himself apt to teach the most humble citizen how to rise to the uppermost echelons of

power never showed the slightest sign of having learned his own lessons. The most he achieved in life was to hold down the same subordinate post for fourteen years, only to then lose said post due to a lack of political foresight. When he did finally manage to earn it back, and only partially, it was by obsequiously currying favor with the new rulers. And after all that sycophancy, he went and died two years later.

2. He had nothing but contempt for intellectuals who, incapable of any political action themselves, attempted to steer the course of events through the written word, but he was never actually anything more than one such intellectual himself.

3. If, in his works, he paints himself as a cold, pessimistic, and malicious observer, in practice, time and again, he revealed himself to be almost pathetically gullible and naive. This professor of calculating opportunism was never able to avail of the opportunities that presented themselves. Carpeaux doesn't mince his words: "He was always on the wrong side."[1] In his youth, he was convinced that Cesare Borgia only did the Papacy's dirty work because he was planning to dethrone the Pope and rule in his stead as the head of a lay government. However well this would have suited Machiavelli's own objectives, it was never in the general's plans or within his capabilities. With his first incarnation of "The Prince" coming to nothing in Borgia, further miscalculations lay in store for our Prophet. After the fall of the Florentine Republic, he clung to the wild hope that the new rulers, whom he had sided against, would allow him to keep his post...in recognition of his loyalty to the fallen regime! Weeks later he

was fired and imprisoned. While in exile, he convinced himself year after year that he could still kowtow his way back into the civil service, but his fawning met only with disdain. Then, at his life's end, sick and broken, pity inspired his former adversaries to restore some of his erstwhile duties, but not even then was he capable of holding onto them. Once again his own imprudence saw him stripped of a post which he would only regain thanks to the charity of others, just before his death.

4. He counseled his Prince to rise to power on the strength of allies and then dispatch them, but he failed to realize that he, a close ally of that Prince, would be one of the first to be put to the sword if their plan worked. He scorned the inventors of ideal governments that never made it off the drawing board, but it apparently never dawned on him that the only reason he still had his head was that *his own* 'ideal government' had failed to materialize.

§

To claim that such a man is a realist, in the strictest meaning of the term, is indefensible. We will soon see the partial sense in which it could be said to apply to him, but whatever that may be, it has to be compatible with the fact that Machiavelli was a Utopian idealist, and not only in terms of political theory, but with regard to his utter lack of any conscious connection between his own theory and practice. The apparent realism with which he accepts the limitations of human action and describes the miseries of politics veils both his prophetic Third Rome

idealism and absolute incapacity to examine his brain-
child from the perspective of his own real position in existence. Hence this need to embody an imaginary character
—the new Moses—and describe the world from the view-
point of this fiction, covering over the depressing reality
that stood in such stark contrast to it. It is precisely this
disconnect between the realms of theoretical construct
and lived experience that I call *cognitive parallax*,
another staple of modern thought. One of the clearest
signs of cognitive parallax is when what an individual
says or writes is disproved by the very fact that he or she
says or writes it: there is no clearer example of this than a
planned Coup d'État that includes, as one of its precepts,
the eradication of its own planner. I will explain this
concept in greater detail further on, but let this brief
outline suffice for the reader to see that the parallax is not
to be confused with conscious lying, hypocrisy or deceit.
Behind the veils, the liar, hypocrite or deceiver believes
wholeheartedly in something. It is in that subjective or
imaginary truth, not the camouflage that conceals it, that
we find the parallax—the disconnect between core beliefs
and the reality of life. Beyond all the hedging, shimmying
and red-herrings of the "Machiavellian" liar lurk the
vestiges of the indelible ingenuity of a man incapable of
truly perceiving his own reality and, moreover, of cross-
referencing its truths with the general convictions
expounded in his published works. Dante Germino asks
why Machiavelli remains for us, in the words of Croce,
"an enigma we shall never unravel." And he provides his
own answer: "Because he was confused, because he was
living through the disintegration of Western civilization

and was part of what Voegelin calls 'The Age of the Great Confusion.'"[2]

However, it would be naive to try to explain Machiavelli through recourse to his "unconscious." As with the liar's paradox, the victim of cognitive parallax is not totally oblivious to himself, but inhabits a twilight zone between truth and falsehood, an overlap in which he is unable to opt entirely for the former, as the lie would then evaporate right before his eyes, or wholly for the latter, because to do so would embrace the lie as the truth of his existence: the only true existence the liar has.

6

THREE WITNESSES

MACHIAVELLI LEFT THREE pieces of testimony that dispel all doubt about the fact that he was quite aware of this ambiguity.

The first is the tale *Belfagor Arcidiavolo*, in which an arch-demon is sent down to Earth to ascertain whether women are really as bad as they say. So, he marries a woman and, mired in debt through her profligacy, ends up being corrupted by humankind. It's a hypertrophic fore-runner to Rousseau: the demon is good by nature, but the social environment he finds himself in debases him. Human evil, on the other hand, has no such excuse, as the devil exercises no influence whatsoever. He is a mere observer, as is Machiavelli, who remains unsullied despite exhorting rulers to embrace the love of lie and violence. He, too, is just an observer of morals.

The reversal of roles is, of course, mere divertissement, but a second text indicates that Machiavelli still believed in it to a point even at death's door. Ill and disabused of any hope of recovery by his doctors, he recounted a dream to some friends:

> I saw an indigent crowd, emaciated, squalid, dressed in rags; I asked them who they were and they replied that they were the Blessed of which spoke the Scriptures: *Beati pauperes quoniam ipsorum est regnum caelorum.*[1] They went upon their way, and there appeared another group, of noble aspect, and richly dressed, and these were engaged in solemn discussion of politics; amongst them I recognized Plato, Plutarch, Tacitus and many other famous figures from classical antiquity. Asked who they were, they responded that they were the Damned, for it is written: *Sapientia huius saeculi inimica est Dei.*[2] When the vision was no more, I was asked with which group I wished to remain. I replied that I would rather discuss politics in Hell with the noble of spirit than be sent to Heaven with the tramps that had first filed past.[3]

The meaning of this dream requires no psychoanalytic interpretation, and is already sufficiently explained by the third item on our list, dated December 10, 1513. The day in question is not to be found circled in calendars, nor does it mark any milestone public occurrence. But it is the date of an essential document in the shift from classical/medieval thought to the "modern" mentality. On that day, Machiavelli, former Second Chancellery secretary, fired soon after the Medici's return to power, exiled to his Tuscan hometown and banned from the Palazzo Vecchio where he had so faithfully served the Republic of Florence for fourteen long years, penned a now famous letter in which he described the misery of his enforced routine:

> In the course of these things comes the hour for dinner, where with my family I eat such food as this poor farm of mine and my tiny property allow. Having eaten, I go back to the inn; there is the host, usually a butcher, a miller, two furnace tenders. With these I sink into vulgarity for the whole day, playing at cricca and at backgammon, and then these games bring on a thousand disputes and countless insults with offensive words, and usually we are fighting over a penny, and nevertheless we are heard shouting as far as San Casciano. So, involved in these trifles, I keep my brain from growing moldy, and satisfy the malice of this fate of mine, being glad to have her drive me along this road, to see if she will be ashamed of it.
>
> On the coming of evening, I return to my house and enter my study; and at the door I take off the day's clothing, covered with mud and dust, and put on garments regal and courtly; and reclothed appropriately, I enter the ancient courts of ancient men, where, received by them with affection, I feed on that food which only is mine and which I was born for, where I am not ashamed to speak with them and to ask them the reason for their actions; and they in their kindness answer me; and for four hours of time I do not feel boredom, I forget every trouble, I do not dread poverty, I am not frightened by death; entirely I give myself over to them.[4]

The first paragraph recounts the moral and intellectual degradation faced by the bureaucrat, the result of losing his position in the State hierarchy. The second celebrates the solace found by the intellectual, who seeks refuge from his external and internal miseries in a few hours spent reading the classics of historiography. Both paragraphs seem quite truthful and accurate: they do indeed correspond to what we know of Machiavelli's life during the period. What does not ring true, however, is the relationship between them.

How can a man so vocationally devoted to the contemplation of the classics and antiquity ("that food which only is mine and which I was born for") disgrace himself gambling and squabbling with the uncouth and unlearned just because he has lost the job that had previously afforded him a good standard of living and the company of the rich? How is it that an intellectual exiled to his home region, and relieved of all bureaucratic duties, does not avail of all that spare time to immerse himself in his studies, as any major philosopher would have done in his place? We know the routines many of them kept. The Academy and Lyceum were open well into the night. Plato and Aristotle only ever stopped studying when it was time for them to teach, and vice-versa. Of all Socrates' many documented conversations, not a single one was on a matter of no consequence. Leibniz devoted every break from his diplomatic duties to the pursuit of science, studying at night and on long journeys. When it came to turning out mathematical treatises and theological expositions, no carriage was too shaky for his inkwell and quill.

Nietzsche had only brief windows of respite from the terrible headaches caused by tertiary syphilis, but he didn't waste them on trifles. He knew he would never be able to work when, or for as long, as he wished, so he learned to compress his intuitions into blazing axioms. Of course, I will say nothing of the rigid discipline of the philosopher monks, the Benedictines or Franciscans, for whom study and teaching were just as much a part of their devotion as prayer and fasting.

So seen in the light of the second paragraph, the first appears strange indeed, and even more unlikely when we read that his daily transfiguration from vulgar cardsharper to companion of Cicero and Livy took nothing but a quick change of clothing—only to revert once again after a night's sleep and a hearty lunch. More jarring still is how a man might switch so swiftly, and by such simple means, from a state of self-destructive, masochistic depression (*I satisfy the malice of this fate of mine, being glad to have her drive me along this road*) to the Olympian tranquility of spiritual communion with the kings, princes and sages of yesteryear. A man does not change personality at the drop of a hat, as if—quite literally—it were a simple change of clothes.

Of course, we could wager that Machiavelli was simply lying, as may well be the case, seeing as he was, by his own admission, a liar.[5] But even if we do assume that the paragraphs are pure invention, why would he invent them precisely *that way*? If the letter does not describe his routine as it was, it therefore describes it as he wanted us to think it was. Why would he want us to imagine his life as an exile in those terms, with such an abrupt and inexplicable shift between two lives—one vulgar, the other noble—in one and the same day? The fiction, if fiction it is, suggests the same enigma as would the fact.

7

PERVERTED NOBILITY

ONE PLAUSIBLE EXPLANATION can be found if we ask ourselves what Machiavelli, dressed "in garments regal and courtly," spoke about with the nobles of antiquity in the inner sanctum of his study, far from the rowdy butchers and millers with whom he had squabbled and slummed away the early afternoon. The question is easy enough to answer, seeing as the idea for *The Prince*, the author's most famous work, was hatched during this period of isolation and is therefore the living result of those imaginary conversations. The book deals with principalities, "what kinds there are, how they can be acquired, how they can be kept, why they are lost." The gist of the teachings the author received from his masters is well known: power is won by wiles and betrayal, maintained by lies and murder, and lost through loyalty and compassion. Morally, it would be hard to put such conduct above those foul-mouthed exchanges around the card table. But the difference between the two worlds Machiavelli inhabited during his routine in exile is certainly not of a moral order. More precisely, it is a matter of degree, from the micro to the macro, from petty contravention to crime in the grandest style. This feeling he had of ascending from a vulgar underbelly to the hallowed sanctuaries of higher thinking was never a shift from corruption to purity, the mundane to the sacred, the base world of ephemeral accident to the Platonic sphere of perfect Forms, but merely a transition from spontaneous wickedness ingrained in ignorance to conscious evil devised, planned and brought to fruition as a work of art. As much as the sages of Antiquity might insist on speaking of other subjects, Machiavelli turns a very selective ear: only his lower self learns, the part attuned to the *sapientia huius saeculi* (wisdom of this world). The inner sanctum to which Machiavelli withdraws from the profanity around him already is, the evidence suggests, the Hell he claimed he would choose over the Heaven of the meek. As Leo Strauss well saw, "To recognize the diabolical character of Machiavelli's thought would mean to recognize in it a perverted nobility of a very high order."[1]

The importance of that passage also lies in what it reveals of the true source of the vision which Machiavelli has of politics: not the pure and objective observation of facts, much less the scientific detachment some of his modern devotees have ascribed to him, but a curious arrangement that allows him to fit cold observations of historical/political details into a wider vision based on the idealized contemplation of demonic malice.

That's why the political models he invented in *The*

Prince and *The Discourses*—the all-powerful ruler and the "Third Rome," respectively—are just imaginary, mythic entities that never materialized historically, no matter how packed they may be with realist detail and even wise generalizations. The Prince is a model of amoral efficiency whose sole historical personification of any relevance was Joseph Stalin, four centuries later in a distant land, and he met with an inglorious end.[2] The second model, the all-powerful State that cut itself adrift from Heaven in order to rule over a vast termite mound of humanity reduced to "absolute earthliness,"[3] saw numerous aborted incarnations over time, and resurged in the 20th Century as the macabre ideal of Antonio Gramsci, but never became anything resembling a reality. It remains, most definitively, an archetype.

It's hard to know whether Machiavelli's description of that period of ostracism is, in a literal sense, real or fictitious. What is certain is that, in either case, it is a reversal of the real meaning of the events. When Machiavelli says that he felt humiliated and embarrassed by his card-playing companions, he does not mean to say that he considered himself superior to them, merely that their badness was far too petty and cheap for his personal aspirations. The ascension from vulgarity to nobility through a daily change of clothes could be misinterpreted as analogous to Rousseau's romantic flight from the stone jungle of the city to the solitude of primordial nature, or, put more generally, as a fussy intellectual's rejection of a stupid world. In fact, what Machiavelli's description does express, and in the clearest possible way, is a counter-initiation in the strict sense in which René Guénon uses the term[4]: of a ritual that allows the simple human sinner to transform into the ascetic of evil; the transfiguration of ignoble passions into spiritualized perversion; the sacrifice of human intelligence for just a few drops of demonic guile.

8

FLEEING EXPERIENCE

WOULD IT HAVE made any sense to call this "realism"?

When Lord Lawrence Arthur Burd wrote that Machiavelli abandoned scholastic argumentation *"secundum Scripturae divinae auctoritatem, Philosophorum dogmata et exempla laudatorum Principum,"*[1] opting instead to cleave to "experience," he added that, in the case of the Italian publicists, "unfortunately, the peculiar character of their experiences often led them to fallacious results, as is seen most clearly in Machiavelli."[2]

But Machiavelli was not limited in that alone. Lord Burd's observation above shows that, for Machiavelli and his companions, divine Scripture, the writings of the philosophers and the most praiseworthy actions of the princes had become dead-letter tropes, fixed doctrinal formulae behind which lay none of the content of inner or outer experience. That's the same as saying that they had no understanding of them whatsoever.

The most convincing proof of that is the unsustainable

and self-contradictory explanation that Machiavelli gives for the success of Moses, to whom he attributes the power of a good armory and *Fortuna*.[3] On one hand, the liberator of the Hebrews had prevailed because he was "an armed prophet," unlike the unarmed Girolamo Savonarola, Machiavelli's contemporary, who failed miserably in his own revolutionary tilt. But Savonarola's problem was never a lack of firepower. He foundered because he was no prophet at all. His decline did not come in the wake of a major battle, but of a public trial by fire that descended into farce. The monk accepted the challenge, but when it came to walking through the flames unscathed to prove the authenticity of his prophetic mission, he sent a surrogate instead, an act which the people duly interpreted as proof that he was a fraud. "In a single day, Savonarola lost the halo of divine prophethood."[4] There's no mention of Moses, weaponry or no weaponry, ever having starred in such a fiasco. The comparison between Savonarola and Moses is forced to the limits of idiocy. But to what end? Machiavelli was not stupid by any means, but he often bets on his readers' stupidity and wins. At first glance, the paragraph appears to laud Moses as a wisely armed prophet and condemn the weaponless Savonarola for his imprudence. But what he actually says is that if Moses had been unmasked as a fraud like the monk in Florence, this would have mattered little, because he had the swords to ensure the success of his prophetic mission anyway. So if Savonarola was revealed to be a pretentious fool, the worst that Moses could have expected was to be reduced to the condition of a pretentious fool with an army.

Calumnious deprecations aside, there's still a problem

here: even if we accept the hypothesis that Moses obtained success by force of arms and not authentic divine charisma, we would still have to ask how he managed to continue being obeyed in death, as the dead, after all, have no legions. Machiavelli would say it all came down to *Fortuna*. The continuity of Judeo-Christendom is due to divine providence, which, as we have seen, Machiavelli identifies with the pure power of uncontrollable chance and elects as the mortal enemy of human will, to be overcome by *Virtù* and the sword. This creates an unresolvable problem. Triumphing through arms, Moses was a champion of *Virtù* fighting against *Fortuna,* whilst simultaneously being assisted by it. The contradiction is so flagrant that not even Machiavelli could ignore it. Nor could he have failed to perceive the falsity of the explanation he throws together for Savonarola's failure, an event he witnessed. He knows perfectly well that he is lying.

On the other hand, it is also clear that the models of the perfect princes proposed by the philosophers and the church were far from just "castles in the air." They only look like that when we bracket out all our knowledge of the structure of the human soul, the passions and temptations, and the "discernment of spirits," etc. The enumeration of the ruler's duties was just a single fragment of the mosaic of moral teachings that held on *duties to the state—* the individual's obligations in accordance with his or her position in society—, itself but a chapter in the even broader framework of morals, woven, in turn, into a formidable fabric of psychological and anthropological experiences and observations that was usually transmitted by scholastic teachings. To contend that some of the most profound scholars of the human soul, such as Saints Augustine and Bernard, produced "castles in the air," ungrounded by direct experience, is an aberration so atrocious that, at first glance, the reader is tempted to explain it away in terms of ignorance of their writings. But just how ignorant could Machiavelli have been of the works of the scholastics and, through these, of the teachings of the Church as a whole? That is a question that does not yet seem sufficiently clarified, but one thing is certain: whole passages from *The Prince* are, formally at least, parodic imitations of the *modus exponendi* of the scholastic treatises, and you cannot parody something you do not know. So, once again, deliberate lying figures as the most viable hypothesis.

Furthermore, how can we admit that the author of *The Prince* was sincere in his condemnation of the philosophers as peddlers of utopias if Plato, Antiquity's chief utopia-spinner, the inventor of the famous "ideal republic," figured amongst the richly-dressed sages of Machiavelli's famous dream, the very group he claimed he would prefer to follow into Hell than ascend to Heaven with the raggedy poor?

How could Machiavelli, turning his back—or at least pretending to do so—on such a rich legacy of experience—possibly have imagined that he was the first to make the transition from the realm of general ideas to the domain of concrete experience? How could he have been so deluded? And if he wasn't deluded, how could he have floated such a brazen lie? The automatic response that he had chosen direct, lived experience of the present over a past known only through the eyes of third parties is

patently false, as he meditates at length over the experience of the Romans as condensed into the works of Titus
Livius, Caesar, Cicero and the like. There are only two
possible explanations for this phenomenon. First: Machiavelli really did not understand the Scriptures, the teachings of the prophets or the laudable examples of the
princes, seeing nothing in that material but empty words
and "airy speculations." Second: he was conceitedly selective, picking and choosing only those ideas that fit with his
secular, amoralist preferences. The two hypotheses are by
no means mutually exclusive: incomprehension and aver-
sion often attract and strengthen each other. But, which-
ever of the two it was, the Judeo-Christian experience was
infinitely ampler in time, space and variety of human and
spiritual situations than the Italic/Roman ever was. By
settling only on the latter, and dismissing the former out of
hand, or reducing it to whatever he had in common with
its baser and more material aspects, Machiavelli narrowed
the horizon of his observations without any legitimate
reason, regulating his selection criteria to suit the political
proposals he aimed to impose. Anthony Parel observes
that:

> One significant way in which Machiavelli contributed to
> the new confidence in man was in his separation of
> politics from religion and his challenge to the secular
> authority of the Church. Such is the essence of his
> secular humanism. The human activity of politics,
> Machiavelli believed, can be isolated from other forms of
> activity and treated in its own autonomous terms. [...] In
> a word, politics can be divorced from theology, and

government from religion. No longer is the State viewed as having a moral end or purpose. Its end is not the shaping of human souls [...], but the creation of conditions which would enable men to fulfill their basic desires for self-preservation, security and happiness. For Machiavelli, religion has the vital function of personal salvation and, from the standpoint of social control, of serving as the foundation for a civic virtue before any moral virtue.[5]

All of that is correct, but the reduction of religion to theology, and of theology to morality, is entirely done on the strength of a personal dogma of Machiavelli's that in no way corresponds to the texts and the facts. Religion per se is not a belief system or moral code (the symbolic obscurity and sheer number of immoral episodes in the Bible should be enough to debunk that illusion immediately). Rather, it is a set of internal and external experiences condensed into symbolic narratives and handed down from generation to generation through a lineage of prophets, apostles and priests, and relived periodically through rites until it slowly, very slowly, consolidates as a system of beliefs and rules that can then, and only then, serve as "an instrument of social control," precisely when the meaning of the experiences that gave rise to it has become too distant in time to be readily reactivated through the experience of personal participation. What's more, if religion can become an instrument of social control, the omnipresence and efficacy of that instrument are too notorious to be abolished *a priori* from any purportedly realist and objective investigation of power. On the other hand, the goals of "self-preservation, security and happiness" toward which political society should strive, according to Machiavelli, so obviously depend on moral and spiritual factors that their exclusion contradicts the terms of the new methodological proposal.

Lastly, there remains one crucial problem: if *Virtù* is the essence of politics, and the mission of *Virtù* is to subjugate *Fortuna*, identified with the will of God, what realism could there possibly be in isolating politics from religion, that is, from knowledge of the enemy, as it were? *Fortuna* is at once the wider backdrop against which politics unfolds *and* the main obstacle politics must overcome. Who would possibly describe as a "realist" a general who draws up a battle plan that willfully ignores the lay of the enemy's territory? Machiavelli seems to believe that all he need do to abolish or neutralize *Fortuna* is turn his back on it. As that is obviously impracticable, any political science worthy of the name, or even a simple practical political wisdom based on common nous, would require, first and foremost, a thorough investigation of *Fortuna* and the limits it imposes upon human action. Only within these limits would it be possible to define *Virtù* and set a reasonable course for its action. Not only does Machiavelli steamroll these obvious facts with the self-confidence of a madman, but, by identifying *Fortuna* with God, he gives no indication whatsoever that he understands that this same step necessarily entails proclaiming the impossibility of separating politics from religion—a separation that is, in fact, the very foundation of his "scientific" project.

Machiavelli's famous realism is not, therefore, realism in any serious sense of the word. It is, perhaps, an idealized realism, selectively cropped to fit the mythic mold of the Prince: a ruler who, cut off from the general conditions of human life and magically leapfrogging millennia of history, reigns supreme over an abstract Italy built especially for him by a philosopher drunk on a mythic vision of ancient Rome. It's on that level that Lord Burd was quite right when he said that "the peculiar character of [Machiavelli and Co.'s] experiences often led them to fallacious results." Perhaps "peculiar" is not the right term: limited, provincial and historically isolated in their experiences rings a lot truer. Even within these limits, if the gaze he turns towards the immediate *modus operandi* of politics might appear "realist" in terms of the critical pessimism and *a priori* exclusion of any higher or holy motivations in human conduct, it is also clearly skewed by a subjective bias deriving from the simple fact that Machiavelli likes the evils he sees and contemplates them with the ecstatic gaze of someone appreciating a work of art. That he is enticed by the intrinsic value of evil and sin, not just their practical applications, is undeniably clear and cannot be concealed behind any purported scientific objectivity.

9

LAYERS OF MEANING

THE NUMBER OF discordant interpretations of Machiavelli's oeuvre reflects the "confusion" Dante Germino was talking about, a befuddlement that lay partially in the historical environment, and partially in the work itself. Someone quite rightly observed that this book repels straightforward interpretations because it is composed of "layers" of meaning. The method of reading in layers was developed, and successfully so, by the phenomenological school in the 20th Century, especially by the Polish philosopher Roman Ingarden, and its application in Machiavelli's case could well prove fruitful.

The layers I can see in Machiavelli are, to an extent, the same as those historically identified by a succession of interpreters. Naturally, they go from the outside in, the accidental to the essential, and the provisional to the lasting, demonstrating that the cumulative labor of critical understanding and discernment undertaken by the various generations was by no means in vain.

1. The immoralism that shocked the earliest readers of *The Prince*, whatever its overall significance in the author's oeuvre (the essence of Machiavelli's thought, or mere wrapping for some deeper idea), was very real indeed and cannot be denied. The reality of "Machiavelli the immoralist" is confirmed in the comedy *La Mandragola* (*The Mandrake*), in which a scurrilous plot involving a husband, a lover and a friar works out well for all concerned, proving that, "in life, the rascals, hypocrites and tricksters have the right idea."[1]

2. The fact that Machiavelli's recommendations were not inventions of his own, but grafted from observation of the political practices he saw going on around him, and backed up by his readings of the Ancients, presents us with a second figure: "Machiavelli the observer." It is true that he was an enthusiastic supporter of the cruelty and malice of a man like Cesar Borgia, whom he took as a model of *Virtù* incarnate. But, just to give some indication of how normal that was for the period, it should be remembered that Borgia was an agent of the Pope, no less, and that a book that would later be added to the notorious *Index librorum prohibitorum* was actually once published under the Papal imprimatur.

3. Machiavelli does not limit himself to description and observation. "Machiavelli the patriot" endeavored to create a formidable compendium of strategies and tactics for achieving an independent Italian state.

4. The observation of "best practices," as it were, allied with his nationalist political plan gave rise to an image of the Ideal Independent State and its likewise ideal ruler, the all-powerful Prince. As Antonio Gramsci notes, "the

utopian character of *The Prince* lies in the fact that the Prince had no real historical existence; [...] but was a pure theoretical abstraction—a symbol of the leader and ideal condottiere."[2] The Prince was, therefore, a foreshadowing of the Sorelian "myth," a utopian image cast upon collective fantasy in order to induce the people to organized action. In this "Machiavelli the myth-maker," the realism of the observation of means blends with the utopian projection of ends.

5. But Machiavelli is not content with observation and myth-making. He bridges the two with sweeping statements about the rise and fall of States, the various conducts of their rulers, matters of national defense, etc. Mixing facts from his own times with those drawn from historical accounts, the resulting generalizations have the structure of a rudimentary political science. This, then, is "Machiavelli the scientist."

6. Neither the ideal Prince nor the independent Italian State turned out anything like the Sorelian myth they were intended to embody. The conditions of the day simply did not allow it. As if somehow foreseeing this disappointing outcome, Machiavelli provided his project with the backdrop of an ampler, longer-term conception: the "Third Rome," the precursor, according to de Sanctis, of the lay modern State. And its creator? "Machiavelli the prophet."

7. The Third Rome is not a copy of the first, but an improved version of it, cured of its fatal flaw: the incapacity to defend itself against the corrosive influence of Judeo-Christendom. In the new State, religion is not entirely vanquished, but subjugated and harnessed to the

Prince's goals.[3] By stressing the novel and futuristic nature of his speculations, Machiavelli is referring precisely to this, and not merely to the personal truculence of the Prince that so shocked the English Cardinal. He is fully aware that he is laying the groundwork for a new civilization, one founded upon the exclusion of all spirituality and, as his disciple Antonio Gramsci would later say, upon the "absolute earthliness" of thought. When he compares himself to a new Moses, he is also cognizant of the parodically inverted character of his endeavor. It's not a matter of parting the Red Sea, but of closing it once and for all, making all escape from his State impossible. This is "Machiavelli the anti-Moses."

8. When Machiavelli confesses that he says nothing he believes and believes nothing he says, he buries any modicum of truth he may once have possessed beneath a mountain of lies. In so doing he shows that all the layers we have examined so far are just veils of camouflage intended to conceal and, at the same time, dialectically reveal the ultimate aim of his project: the advent of the post-Christian or anti-Christian State. He doesn't care about any of the rest. The means may be moral, amoral or immoral, it matters not. The packaging of his discourse could be chronicle, science, myth, defamation, praise, or outright lying, it's all the same. The State that comes to fruition might be a monarchy, a republic or a blend of the two, and its government tyrannical, democratic or half-and-half—that's immaterial. Italy can split from the Vatican or make the Vatican its seat in order to hollow it out from the inside, he doesn't mind. It's all just a matter of convenience—hence the impression of neutrality, balance

and realism, not to mention the impossibility of reducing Machiavelli's thought to a fixed doctrinal formula, because all of its antagonistic elements will not be reabsorbed into some theoretical conclusion, but into a final objective that is the only indispensable factor in all of this, and the one true purpose everything else must serve: the eradication of *Fortuna* in favor of *Virtù;* the subjugation of God to a human will that has freely chosen Hell over Heaven. Toward that end, all is permitted, even to jumble the very meanings of the words *Virtù* and *Fortuna*, painting the former as brute force one minute, and as the disciplined conduct of the citizenry the next, and the latter as casual fortuity here, and as divine providence there, separating or mixing the senses depending on whether he wishes to use the truth as camouflage or camouflage as the ambiguous expression of a truth that can always be denied later.[4] In short, anything goes: so long as all roads lead to his Third Rome. That the plan of this undertaking could be revealed only through a complex system of blind alleys, disguises, and apparent or actual paradoxes has nothing whatsoever to do with fear of ecclesiastic vengeance, all but unthinkable in a time of chic Neo-paganism, but to the very nature of the project itself, which, inspired by the founding lie of "absolute secularization and earthliness," could not be expressed other than in a language of chiaroscuro and self-contradiction. In fact, the contradictions are so abundant they have left generations of readers in a tizzy. They are not only inherent to the work itself, but detectable, too, in its historical antecedents and in the later development of events. Two examples will illustrate this clearly. On one hand, chief amongst the inspirations for Machiavelli's

Third-Rome plan was the senseless hope that Cesar Borgia, an agent of Papal authority, would topple the Pope and install a lay State at the Vatican. Not only did the famous Duke fail to do any of that, he ended his days in disgrace, showing that malice and brutishness do not have the practical omnipotence Machiavelli had claimed for them. On the other hand, the only lay State that, with any approximation of Machiavelli's model—that is, of a mixed aristocratic/democratic regime—, ever managed to take hold and last for any length of time is the United States of America. But with one essential difference: far from wishing to harness Christianity to its worldly ends, the American State steeped itself in Biblical influences and, as Alexis de Tocqueville quite rightly pointed out, took the Judeo-Christian ethic as one of its constitutive pillars. The fact that the formal conception of the Machiavellian State, without doubt a stroke of wizardry in itself, took the form of a Christian State and not its opposite, as Machiavelli had planned, is one of those ironies of history that remind us that, at the end of the day, the devil is a servant of God. What we have here is "Machiavelli the satanist," who knows exactly who he's working for and can only admit as much in a doubly ironic manner: before the devout masses, he appeals to false demonstrations of piety in order to make it look like he's serving God, when he knows he toils for the devil; and then, when in the presence of anti-Christian high-rollers, makes like he's working for the devil when he knows perfectly well that his malign oeuvre, when all is said and done, unfolds *ad majorem Dei gloriam* (For the greater glory of God).

According to his son Piero, then thirteen, on his

deathbed Machiavelli confessed his sins to a friar and passed away in the grace of God. We don't know if this is true or not, or whether his repentance was sincere, or merely the final act in a bitter comedy whose *dramatis personae*, surviving their author, strut the world's stage to this day.

10

PARODIC INVERSION OF
CHRISTIANITY

MOVING FROM THE center to the fringes, we will try to grasp the internal order in Machiavelli's work as it was developed over time.

Ostracized from the halls of power, reduced to the solitude of a mediocre life, the Florentine former-secretary came up with a new formula for government that could seduce the rulers of his day, and the various pretenders to their thrones, and therefore win some favor for this competent staffer so abruptly excluded from the business of State. The most enticing aspect of this formula is the way it releases these rulers from the moral and psychic fetters of religion. Machiavelli has duly noted the conflict between the ruling elite and the priestly caste—a recurrent theme since the dawn of time and rife with mythical resonances, such as the traditional she-bear and boar symbolism[1]—then manifesting in a particularly jagged form as nation States attempted to emerge out of the long-cast shadow of the old ecclesiastic project for a European

Empire. And it seems he has found a way to meddle in that conflict, coming down so heavily on the side of the nobility that they could not possibly deny him due recompense.

The plan is two-tier, corresponding to the author's two most important books, *The Prince* (1513) and *Discourses on the First Decade of Titus Livius* (1517). The first focuses on the more pressing issue of attaining absolute power, and sets forth the ideal of the prince capable of delivering this new status quo. The second broadens the scope of the plan ambitiously, and the body of historical references used to support it: the local principality gives way to a universal republic, and the plan for Italian independence to the utopia of a new world order.

The reasoning Machiavelli presents to justify the subjugation and ultimate destruction of the Church by the ascendant nobility also unfolds in two stages. In *The Prince*, it appears under the form of a practical immoralism that exempts the ruler from any moral obligations imposed by Christianity. In *Discourses*, the demolition of the Church is taken to a whole new level with the complete and calumnious falsification of Church history and the construction of a model of the State founded upon the parodic inversion of Christianity.

The first of these aspects is known high and low and needs no further elucidation, and the second, while far more interesting, does not require exhaustive treatment either, as the general arguments Machiavelli lodges against the Church have already been hashed out in the literature. What really concerns us in the present chapter is the tactic Machiavelli uses to make these moves work. It basically comes down to taking praise, slander and ambiguity and mixing it all up into a confusion so dense that the reader, unable to glean a clear doctrinal formula that might encapsulate the author's thought, can only woozily and fuzzily endorse the Machiavellian project, trusting, as de Sanctis said, that it is, in fact, the project of modernity —a contention none could reasonably oppose without going against what consensus considered an inevitable historical necessity.

We shall take a look at some examples of how Machiavelli goes about causing this confusion. To start with, he admits that religion is useful to the maintenance of the State, and commends the legislator Numa for having introduced the religious institutions to the structure of the Roman State, as these had enabled him to secure the people's obedience on the promise of heavenly reward when he had neither the earthly punishments nor prizes with which to obtain the same result. He recognizes that Christianity played the very same role in the origin of the European governments and could continue to do so quite usefully in the future State, as a "positive factor in the exaltation of patriotism, the creation of civic virtues indispensable to life and to the defense of the State."[2] In addition to some perfunctory plaudits that appear here and there in Machiavelli's writings, this idea would seem to presume a benevolent and even conservative conception of religion. But it jars so utterly with his apology for the use of anti-Christian methods in the art of governance that one has to ask what vestiges of Christianity could possibly remain in a religion reduced in this way to an instrument of the State. On the other hand, as Machiavelli resolutely asserts—and in this he got the jump on Kant and positivism—that we lack sufficient knowledge of "things natural and supernatural" to be able to factor religious doctrines into the interpretation of human affairs, concluding, as a result, that politics should be approached in total independence of any theological considerations, it is evident that whatever residual Christianity might linger in the future State ought to be relegated to the very function Numa had afforded religion in general: to dupe the masses into obedience through the "Machiavellian" manipulation of illusory beliefs.[3] As Machiavelli sees it, Christianity's greatest quality is its utility as a con, and he spares no praise for that application. However, when held up to true Christianity, his distortion comprises what is perhaps the most slanderous attack the faith had ever sustained. Faced with apparent contradictions, the reader is left wondering whether Machiavelli was pro-Christian or anti-Christian, but cannot shake the feeling that he regarded treating the religion as a handy fraud as not only acceptable, but perhaps even praiseworthy for its "neutrality" and "balance."

Elsewhere in the *Discorsi*, Machiavelli seems to defend the Church, and even more vigorously than before, when he declares that the problem does not lie with Christianity itself, but with a decadent version of it, spawned by a clergy enriched by extortion and corrupted by idleness. This appeal to a return to a primitive Christianity sounds deceptively pious, as would an identical call issued centuries later by Liberation Theology. The passage is worth examining in full:

These miracles were common enough in Rome, and among others this was believed, that when the Roman soldiers were sacking the city of Veii, certain of them entered the temple of Juno and spoke to the statue of the goddess, saying, *"Wilt thou come with us to Rome?"* when to some it seemed that she inclined her head in assent, and to others that they heard her answer, *"Yea."* For these men being filled with religious awe (which Titus Livius shows us by the circumstance that, in entering the temple, they entered devoutly, reverently, and without tumult), persuaded themselves they heard that answer to their question, which, perhaps, they had formed beforehand in their minds. [...] Had religion been maintained among the princes of Christendom on the footing on which it was established by its Founder, the Christian States and republics would be far more united and far more prosperous than they now are; nor can we have surer proof of its decay than in witnessing how those countries which are the nearest neighbours of the Roman Church, the head of our faith, have less devoutness than any others; so that anyone who considers its earliest beginnings and observes how widely different is its present practice, might well believe its ruin or its chastisement to be close at hand.[4]

But what exactly were the "earliest beginnings" of Christianity? It cannot mean the practice of the Evangelical virtues in the strict sense, as Machiavelli detested them. Nor can it mean the revelation of the supernatural, as of this, he claims, we have no knowledge. The quality par excellence of Christianity in its primordial form can only have been its capacity to work miracles, albeit in the Roman rather than Christian sense of the term. In other words, not authentic divine interventions in the course of worldly events, but appearances which the credulous faithful have a propensity to interpret as such, much like the Roman soldiers did in Juno's temple. In short, primitive Christianity had a knack of tricking souls into obedience. The problem with decadent Christianity is not its laxity with regard to the Evangelical virtues, but its loss of the capacity to hoodwink the masses. No matter how deftly the blasphemy conceals itself beneath a mountain of disguises, it cannot have escaped Machiavelli, who adds insult to injury by attributing this mastery of the dark arts of deceit to Christ himself, whilst lamenting its later loss by incapable disciples. And it is to this Christ, transformed into a Machiavellian politician, that the Florentine directs his devotion, despite pretending all the while to praise the Christ of the Gospels.

This intentional parodic reversal becomes even more evident when, in *Discourses*, Machiavelli revives his discussion of the fledgling and still unstable principality. What should the newly installed ruler do to consolidate his power? The answer is he should radicalize the novelty of the situation by suddenly turning everything inside-out. The best thing to do is "employ new men, and like David when he became king, exalt the humble and depress the great, *'filling the hungry with good things, and sending the rich away empty.'*"[5]

There are three highly significant details in this paragraph. First: it contains the only Biblical quotation in the whole book. Second: it draws on the actions of a Biblical

king in order to illustrate the ideal conduct of the new
prince, but does so with reference to the New Testament
treatment of the story (Luke 1: 53), not the Old Testament
account (2 Samuel, 5: 1-16). It is therefore taken entirely
out of the context of King David's life and rise. Third:
there is nothing in the story of David to suggest he did
anything resembling what Machiavelli recommends to his
prince. Quite the contrary, in fact: the prophet Nathan
accuses him of exploiting the poor and sparing the rich. If
anyone in the New Testament is said to turn such tables it
is neither prince nor king, but God himself, according to
Machiavelli's own quote: *Esurientes implevit bonis et
divites dimisit inanes,* in the original Latin. The words are
spoken by Mary after the Assumption, and they celebrate
God's choice of a poor and simple peasant woman to be
the Mother of his Son. Of course, she was not referring to
a reversal of the socioeconomic hierarchy here, as the priv-
ilege invested in the Holy Virgin cannot be socialized
among the poor or seized by the rich. In short, the episode
Machiavelli uses to back up his counsel has nothing whatsoever to do with that counsel; the passage evoked to illustrate the episode has nothing at all to do with that episode;
and the words quoted to explain the episode and the
meaning of the advice have nothing in the least to do with
either.

Some readers will almost automatically assume that
the whole imbroglio was caused by a simple flub, but that
hypothesis does not hold water, not least because it would
require taking the ever-meticulous Machiavelli for a
monster of sloppiness, but also because the quotation is
given in Latin, and with literal precision.

This triple smokescreen, blown to befuddle the reader careless enough not to check the sources, shows exactly what Machiavelli meant when he said that he concealed the truth beneath so many layers of lies it became impossible to find. The truth in this case is that the Prince, eager to tighten his hold over his new seat, ought to impose an upending of the social order as a new miracle of the Annunciation, turning himself not into a new David, but a new God the Father, creator and renewer of all things.

To make matters even worse, Machiavelli admits that the methods to which the Prince ought to resort can indeed be so cruel and violent as to become "contrary not merely to every Christian, but to every civilized rule of conduct."[6] In short, the Prince should claim God's authority for himself and do so in full awareness that this God is the enemy of Christians and of humanity as a whole. Otherwise put, he should make imitating the devil the new form of imitating God, whilst posing before the masses as a new God and making them believe that they are worshipping God when they kneel before the Devil-Prince.

If that is not diabolism in its purest state—and in an incomparably more perverse sense than the "material" immoralism of *Raison d'État* already identified by the critics—then we must seriously revise our definition of the devil.

11

THE PARADOX

Conscious of the radically anti-Christian character of his utopia, as Machiavelli lay upon his deathbed he confessed his sins, received the last rites, and died under the blessings of the Church, but without ever having publicly disavowed a single word he had said. Of course, this presents a problem, but that problem is, once again, the liar's paradox. Was Machiavelli lying when he confessed, or was he sincerely confessing a life of lies and blasphemy? Put in these terms, we simply can't say. God alone can know. Luckily, you don't have to be God to tell the difference between subjective sincerity and objective self-knowledge. Machiavelli may have been subjectively sincere when he made his confession, but that does not mean he had any real notion of the true measure of his actions, much less clearly understood the existential correlation between actions and words. Given the disconnect between the "Machiavellian" content of Niccolò's works and his conduct in political practice, marked as it was by his clueless devotion to the powerful, this latter hypothesis can be dismissed out of hand. Much harder to eliminate is the possibility that he actually saw his writings as political acts, but even if he did, we find nothing grandiose or demonic at all in their aims, just the pedestrian ambition of a man trying to get his job back. The mismatch in scale between this personal goal and the unbridled power Machiavelli offers to ambitious (aspiring) rulers is so enormous that to countenance it we would have to presume a seismic rift between "life" and "work." In order to accompany Machiavelli's discourse with the minimum credulity required not to dismiss it all as psychotic ramblings, we cannot really expect to find any ground in lived experience—whether his, our own, or of some historical other. We have to read him with a liberal dose of the suspension of disbelief which Coleridge asked of the reader of an imaginative work.

That Machiavelli was not a political scientist endeavoring to draw objectively valid conclusions from a sufficiently ample pool of facts has already been exhaustively demonstrated by Maurizio Viroli.[1] The evidence presented is the overwhelming preponderance of rhetorical argument over any logical/dialectical proof in either *The Prince* or the *Discourses*.

But this rhetorical argumentation hangs on a compositional interconnection of four elements: the *background* or context, the *judge* or listener, the *discourse* in itself (form and content), and the *aim* it is designed to achieve.[2] And yet, the fact remains that these four components do not work together, or for each other, at all in Machiavelli's works. From the outset, the objective is dual—part public, part private—but not twofold, as the greater annuls rather than enables the lesser. Acceptance of the proposed plan by the ruler to whom it is addressed does not imply, and is not conditioned upon, any agreement on his part to restore the author to his former position, though the recovery of that job is, we're told, the author's personal goal. In fact, the opposite is true: that very plan, if carried through, would inevitably put the author's life in danger. Hardly less ambiguous than the goal is the background: Machiavelli waits until he has been booted from the halls of power to put himself in the ruler's shoes, and think from his perspective, even if that means defending the point of view of the very forces that scuppered his own career. How was he able to step so far outside of his own skin and so close to those he had such obvious reasons to hate? He answered that question himself in his December 1513 letter to Francesco Vettori: in order to think like the princes and kings, he detached himself from his own life and dressed like them, then transported himself into another world by power of the imagination. That this world pertained to those condemned to Hell (though that in no way diminished their elegance and nobility) was something he was keenly aware of, and admitted as much on his deathbed. But his decision to follow them into that Hell is something his Christian death only days later obliges us to consider, as his competent biographer Roberto Ridolfi points out, nothing but the final jest of a lifelong jester.[3] The kings and princes can go to the devil all they wish. The more prudent Machiavelli sends for Friar Mateus and has him administer the last rites.

Machiavelli's rhetoric would therefore not seem to

have a rhetorical aim, other than in the highly ambiguous sense of the nominal goal not being the author's actual objective at all. Niccolò sells his reader-prince a plan, a strategy and a system full of justifications that he does not buy himself—in life or, it transpires, in death.

Soon after publishing the *Discorsi* (1517), Machiavelli lost interest in the political musings of Antiquity. His commentary on Titus Livy stalled at the first decade and went no further. Its author devoted the whole of the following year to theatrical and philological pursuits, and the rest of his life to histories of Italy, interrupted only by a brief period in which he completed *The Art of War* (1521), a tardy wrap-up of the conclusions drawn from his time organizing the Florentine army.

It is therefore doubtful that he took those cogitations vitally seriously, as he neither applied them nor expanded upon them. That does not mean he scorned them. While writing them, he would lapse into a state of self-aggrandizement in which he saw himself as a daring pioneer, a trailblazer of the future, and even a new Moses parting the *mare magnum* of the power struggles between the priestly caste and the nobility. But that done, he forgot it all and went back to his bureaucratic brief as a mid-ranking civil servant and family breadwinner going about his duties to this world and the next.

In short, Machiavelli neither believed nor disbelieved what he said. The distinction simply does not apply in his case. He wandered perfectly at ease among truths and falsehoods, with the freedom of the artist who delights in his creations without the least concern for the effects they may have on the real world, or even needing to understand them in any intellectually relevant way. His oeuvre is neither a political philosophy nor a political science, but a simulation of both. It is not a rhetorical exhortation, but the simulation of one, and it targets an outcome altogether different to that which his discourse presents to its readers. And it is not a parody of the morals and manners of his day either. Parodies always have a moral foundation, but Machiavelli floats between condemning political hardball in the name of morality and condemning morality in the interests of an idealization of the very worst proclivities of statecraft. From beginning to end, it offers a fictional speculation, a musing on the possible that makes no attempt whatsoever to stand apart from either the true or the probable, but to appear, and with extreme skill, the real deal. It is, therefore, a poetic simulation of rhetoric in precisely the same way as the speeches of Caesar, Brutus or Henry V in Shakespeare, with the only difference being that Machiavelli's simulation was crafted in such a way as to make its target readers take it for authentic rhetorical discourse. If, during the course of its composition, the author occasionally managed to convince himself of the justice of the cause he pretended to defend, it never stopped him from walking an altogether different walk, and of disavowing the whole thing in those final moments, when he confessed his sins to the same God he had bombarded with blasphemies.

ABOUT THE AUTHOR

Olavo de Carvalho was born in Campinas, São Paulo State, on April 29, 1947. He has been hailed by the critics as one of the most original and audacious Brazilian thinkers in activity. His work defends human interiority against the tyranny of collective authority, especially when harnessed to a "scientific" ideology. For Olavo de Carvalho, there is an unbreakable link between the objectivity of knowledge and the autonomy of individual consciousness, a bond that gets lost to us when the validity of knowledge is reduced to an impersonal and uniform checklist for use by the academic community.

www.olavodecarvalho.com

Take a moment to visit the Philosophy Seminar.

The Seminar is, first and foremost, a philosophy course designed to help students practice philosophy rather than simply repeat what others have said about it. The Seminar is also an integral education system open to various fields of knowledge, including literature, the arts, communication and expression, and the natural sciences.

www.seminariodefilosofia.org

Follow Olavo on Social:

Telegram | t.me/opropriolavo (Preferred)

facebook.com/carvalho.olavo
twitter.com/opropriolavo
instagram.com/opropriolavodecarvalho

NOTES

Author's Note

1. *The Originality of Machiavelli,* Isaiah Berlin, G. C. Sansoni editore, 1972, 206 pages.

1. The Obscurity of Modern Philosophy

1. Giovanni Reale, *Toward a New Interpretation of Plato,* Catholic University of America Press, 10th ed. 1997
2. *Fashionable Nonsense,* Alan Sokal and Jean Bricmont, Picador, USA 1997.
3. Literally: "About you the tale is told."

2. Image of Machiavelli

1. Giovanbattista Busini, cit. Maurizio Viroli, *Machiavelli,* Oxford University Press, 1998, p. 114
2. Lauro Escorel, *Introdução ao Pensamento Político de Maquiavel,* Rio de Janeiro, Simões, 1958, p. 90
3. See Friedrich Meinecke, *Machiavellism: the Doctrine of Raison d'Etat and its Place in Modern History,* Routledge, 2017.
4. "Ever since Niccolò Machiavelli's day *The Prince* has been considered by some to be a diabolical production, and its author's name has been held synonymous with Satan (hence, according to Samuel Butler, 'Old Nick'). Passages have been quoted out of context to prove their author depraved and immoral. Although such a practice is unfair and does not do justice to Machiavelli's whole thesis. It must be admitted that he exalts the state above the individual; that the most enthusiastic exponents of his theories have been Napoleon, Bismarck, Hitler, Mussolini, and Stalin; and that his state is exempt from the obligations of 'religion' and 'morality.'" (Buckner B. Trawick, *World Literature,* 1962).

5. *De Legationibus Libri Tres* was Gentili's first treatise on international law, published in 1585.

6. Maurizo Viroli's term.

7. 'According to the authority of the divine Scriptures, the affirmations of the philosopher and the example of praiseworthy princes.' St. Thomas Aquinas, Argument *of De Regimine Principum.*

8. Cit. Escorel, 1958, p. 3 note 1

9. Ernst Cassirer, *The Myth of the State*, Hamburg, Meiner, 1946, re-ed 2007, pp. 152-155

10. Otto Maria Carpeaux, "Inteligência de Maquiavel," in *Ensaios Reunidos*, 1942-1978. De "A Cinza do Purgatório" até "Livros na Mesa." Rio de Janeiro: Topbooks/UniverCidade, 1999, Vol 1, pp. 778-9. The reference is to L. Olschki's *Machiavelli the Scientist* (Berkeley, 1945, re-ed 1948).

11. Pasquale Villari, Niccolò Machiavelli e i suoi tempi. Ilustrati con nuovi documenti, Volume III, Firenze: Successori Le Monnier, 1882, p. 379. Translation from book available at <https://archive.org/details/niccolomachi-aveloo01vill/page/378/mode/2up> Accessed on Sept. 19, 2020.

12. Citations from Pietro Caporilli, "Le lezione del 'segretario fiorentino' nella politica di Mussolini e Napoleone" , s.d. Available at <http://classicweb.archive.org/web/20041213181607/http://www.carpe-diem.it/cultura/htm/macc.htm> Accessed on May 13, 2011.

13. Cf. Anne Lyon Haight and Chandler B. Grannis, *Banned Books 387 BC to 1978 AD*, New York and London: R.R. Bowker Co., 1978.

14. "The individual tends to be in constant flight. Always breaking the law, evading taxes, refusing to go to war. Few are those—be they heroes or saints—who sacrifice their egos on the altar of the State. They are forever on the cusp of revolt against the State."

    In the original: *L'individuo tende ad evadere continuamente. Tende a disubbidire alle leggi, a non pagare i tributi, a non fare la guerra. Pochi sono coloro—eroi o santi—che sacrificano il proprio io sull'altare dello Stato. Tutti gli altri sono in stato di rivolta potenziale contro lo Stato."* ("Preludio al Machiavelli," in Gerarchia, April 1924, Scritti e Discorsi, vol. IV, p. 109).

15. Available at <http://www.marxists.org/archive/trotsky/germany/1933/330610.htm>. Accessed on. Sept. 19, 2020

16. See Benedetto Croce, *Aesthetic as Science of Expression and General Linguistic*, Library of Alexandria, 2012.

17. Carpeaux, *Ensaios Reunidos*, vol I, 1999, p. 779.

18. Cit. in John Bowle, *Politics and Opinion in the Nineteenth Century: An Historical Introduction*, New York, Oxford University Press, 1954, p. 356.

19. Friedrich Meinecke, *Machiavellism: the Doctrine of Raison D'Etat and its Place in Modern History*, trans. Douglas Scott, New Haven, Yale University Press, 1957, p.26

20. See Friedrich Nietzsche *Human, All Too Human* § 224.

21. Francesco di Sanctis, *Storia della Letteratura Italiana*, Firenze, Editore Salani, 1965, p. 110. In the original: "*È il programma del mondo moderno, sviluppato, corretto, ampliato, più o meno realizzato. E sono grandi le nazioni che più vi si avvicinano. Siamo dunque alteri del nostro Machiavelli. Gloria a lui, quando crolla alcuna parte dell'antico edificio. E gloria a lui, quando si fabbrica alcuna parte del nuovo.*"

22. Leo Strauss, *Thoughts on Machiavelli*, Chapter 1, Chicago, The University of Chicago Press, 1958.

23. See Vicki B. Sullivan, *Machiavelli's Three Romes. Religion, Human Liberty and Politics Reformed.* De Kalb (Illinois): Northern Illinois University Press. 1996.

24. Other "prophets" he lists alongside Moses are Cyrus, Theseus and Romulus, a clear indication that his notion of the concept underscores command, regardless of the cognitive aspect that is key to the religious acceptation of the term.

25. Leo Strauss, *Thoughts on Machiavelli*, 1958, p. 36

26. *Id., ibid.*

27. Garrett Mattingly, "Machiavelli's Prince: Political Science or Political Satire?," in *The American Scholar* 27 (1958): 482-491.

28. *Id., ibid.*

29. Viroli, 1998, chapter 5.

3. Machiavelli's Pseudo-Realism

1. Strauss, 1958, pp. 223-225.

2. "Hegel was, of course, obsessed with the political weakness of Germany, living in the Napoleonic period of collapse, of negation, he hoped, following the dialectic, for the reaction, the reaffirmation of German might. He aspired, Dr. Sabine believes, to be the

Machiavelli of a new Germany"(John Bowie, *Politics and Opinions in the Nineteenth Century: An Historical Introduction*, New York, Oxford University Press, 1954, p. 43).

3. Eric Voegelin, On Hegel: A Study in Sorcery, in *The Collected Works of Eric Voegelin* (12): *Published Essays 1966-1985*, ed. Ellis Sandor, Baton Rouge and London, Louisiana University Press, 1990, pp. 213-255.

4. Eric Voegelin, *The Collected Works of Eric Voegelin* (22): *History of Politica Ideas vol. 4, Renaissance and Reformation*, chap 1, with an introduction by David L. Morse and William M. Thompson, Missouri, University of Missouri Press.

5. Dante Germino, "Was Machiavelli a 'Spiritual Realist'?" In: ERIC VOEGELIN SOCIETY MEETING 2000, Panel 2, Washington: Eric Voegelin Society 2000, available at https://siteso1.lsu.edu/faculty/voegelin/wp-content/uploads/sites/80/2015/09/Germino1.pdf, accessed on October 19, 2020.

5. The Liar

1. Otto Maria Carpeaux, *História da literatura ocidental,* I-A, Rio de Janeiro: Edições O Cruzeiro, 1961, p. 485.

2. Germino, 2000, *loc. cit.*

6. Three Witnesses

1. *Blessed are the poor, for theirs is the Kingdom of Heaven.*

2. *For the wisdom of this world is foolishness in God's sight.*

3. Translated from Escorel, 1958, pp. 82-83.

4. Available at http://courses.washington.edu/hsteu401/Letter%20%20to%20Vettori.pdf, accessed on November 20, 2020.

5. Cit. In Strauss, 1958, p.36.

7. Perverted Nobility

1. Strauss, 1958, p. 13

2. See the pathetic description of Stalin's last moments in Dmitri Volkogonov's *Stalin: Triumph and Tragedy,* Grove Weidenfeld, 1991

3. Antonio Gramsci's full words were "the absolute secularization and earthliness of thought."

4. See René Guénon, *Le Régime de la Quantité et lês Signes des Temps*, Paris, Gallimard, 1946, re-ed 1972.

8. Fleeing Experience

1. "...according to the authority of Holy Writ and the teachings of the philosophers as well as the practice of worthy princes." St. Thomas Aquinas, *On Kingship to the King of Cyprus*, Address to the King of Cyprus.

2. Lord Lawrence Arthur Burd, *Il Principe*, Oxford, Clarendon Press, 1891 p. 283

3. "Hence it is that all armed prophets have conquered, and the unarmed ones have been destroyed. Besides the reasons mentioned, the nature of the people is variable, and whilst it is easy to persuade them, it is difficult to fix them in that persuasion. And thus it is necessary to take such measures that, when they believe no longer, it may be possible to make them believe by force.

If Moses, Cyrus, Theseus, and Romulus had been unarmed they could not have enforced their constitutions for long—as happened in our time to Fra Girolamo Savonarola, who was ruined with his new order of things immediately the multitude believed in him no longer, and he had no means of keeping steadfast those who believed or of making the unbelievers to believe."

Machiavelli, Niccolò, *The Prince*, Chapter VI - Concerning new principalities which are acquired by one's own arms and ability

4. Escorel, 1958, p. 24.

5. Anthony Parel, ed. *The Political Calculus: Essays on Machiavelli's Philosophy Toronto*: University of Toronto Press, 1972. p. 38

9. Layers of Meaning

1. Carpeaux, *História da literatura ocidental,* 1961, p. 483

2. Antonio Gramsci, "The Modern Prince," *Selections from The Prison Notebooks*, Lawrence & Wishart Ltd. p. 126.

3. A project that would be taken up again, and quite literally, in theory, by Antonio Gramsci, and in practice, by systematic kgb

infiltration into Catholic hierarchy, giving rise to "the theology of liberation." See Ricardo de la Cierva, *Las Puertas del Infierno. La Historia de la Iglesia Jamás Contada*, Toledo, Editorial Fénix, 1995, and *La Hoz y la Cruz. Auge y Caída del Marxismo y la Teologia de la Libertación,* id, 1996.

4. For example, in *Discourses*, 1-4: "Né si può chiamare in alcun modo con ragione una repubblica inordinata, dove sianno tanti esempli di virtù: perché li buoni esempli nascano dalla buona educazione, la buona educazione, dalle buone leggi," and, in 1-10, "quelli che in stato privato vivono in una repubblica, o che per fortuna o per virtù né diventono principi..."

"Nor can we reasonably pronounce that city ill-governed wherein we find so many instances of virtue; for virtuous actions have their origin in right training, right training in wise laws [...]" and, in 1-10, "that those who live in a private state in a republic or who either by fortune or by virtù become princes of it..."

10. Parodic Inversion of Christianity

1. See René Guénon, *Symboles de la Science Sacreé*, Paris, Gallimard, 1962, chapter 24.
2. Escorel, 1958, p. 125.
3. *Discorsi*, Book I, LVI. Translated by Ninian Hill Thomson, London, Kegan Paul, Trench & Co. 1883
4. *Discorsi*, Book I, XII. Id. My reading of this paragraph accompanies that which Anthony J. Parel makes in *The Machiavellian Cosmos*, New Haven, Yale University Press, 1992, p. 47, and endorsed by Sullivan, op. cit. pp 38-39. Sullivan concludes that: "Machiavelli simultaneously expresses an impious admiration for the pagan understanding and covers that impiety up under the altogether inappropriate guise of an appeal to primitive Christianity...."
5. *Discorsi*, Book I, XXVI. Id.
6. *Discorsi*, Book I, XXVI. Id.

11. The Paradox

1. Mauricio Viroli, *Machiavelli*, Oxford and New York, Oxford University Press, 1998.

2. See Olavo de Carvalho, *Aristóteles em Nova Perspectiva, Introdução à Teoria dos Quatro Discursos*, São Paulo, É Realizações.
3. Roberto Ridolfi, *The Life of Niccolò Machiavelli*, University of Chicago Press, 1964

INDEX

Printed in Great Britain
by Amazon

38046209R00066